ALONG
THE CHILTERN
WAYS

G. R. Crosher

CASSELL · LONDON

CASSELL & COMPANY LTD
35 Red Lion Square, London WC1R 4SG
Sydney, Auckland, Toronto,
Johannesburg

First published 1973

ISBN 0 304 29193 5

Printed in Great Britain by
Northumberland Press Limited,
Gateshead
F.673

Contents

Illustrations

The photographs of West Wycombe (*No. 13*), Watlington (*No. 22*), Mapledurham (*No. 24*) and Wendover (*No. 27*) are by A. G. Crosher; all the other photographs are by W. R. Crosher.

To
F.A.C.
with love
and
W.S.C.
in memoriam

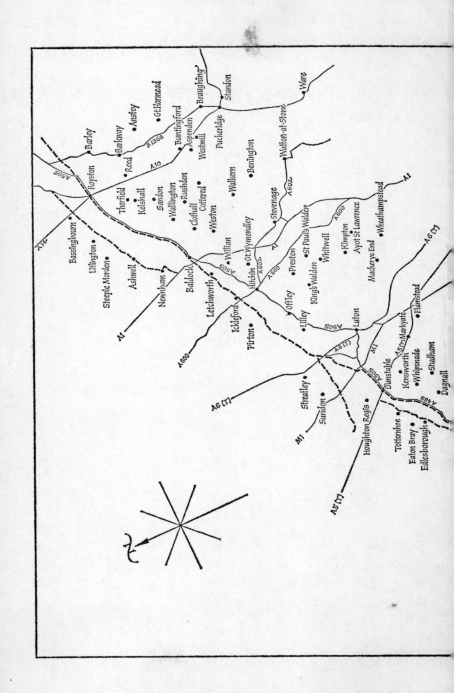

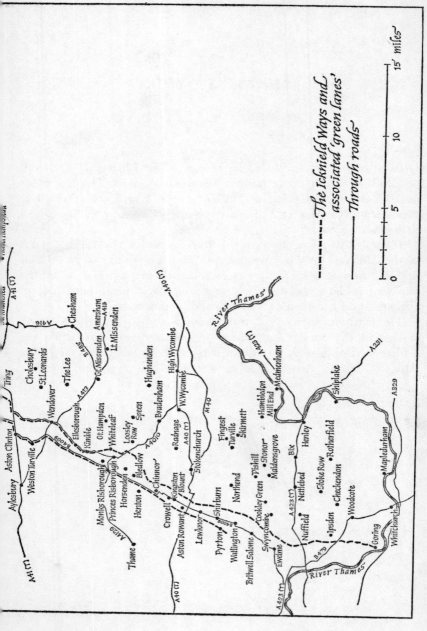

The Icknield Ways and associated 'green lanes'
Through roads

0   5   10   15 miles

© _Cassell & Co. Ltd., 1973_

Author's Note

Ordnance Survey one-inch Sheets 159 (The Chilterns) and 147 (Bedford & Luton) cover most of the Chiltern area. The few miles of Icknield from Goring to Ipsden are on Sheet 158 (Oxford & Newbury); Royston and the area south of it are on Sheet 148 (Saffron Walden).

Though this book covers many ways by which the varying parts of the Chilterns may be approached, those who prefer to go on foot will be interested in the series of footpath maps prepared by the Chiltern Society. To date they cover mainly the southern half of the area and are obtainable from local booksellers.

The Chiltern Society also publishes, bi-monthly, 'Chiltern News', telling of the Society's activities on behalf of all who enjoy the Chilterns. Copies may be obtained from the general secretary, P. S. Mould, Season's Watch, Bledlow Ridge, High Wycombe, Bucks.

Postscript

as Introduction

Though I did not have the luck to be born within the Chilterns, my acquaintance with the region goes back to childhood. Among my earlier recollections are week-long visits to family friends who ran a farm near the Missendens; during my teens, on foot or by cycle I ventured further and found the southerly area within the Thames loop; and, having for the past twenty years lived in Hertfordshire, my Chiltern acquaintance has spread into the very different and often less regarded country about the Icknield Ways and the old roads to Cambridge. So, when the opportunity came to write about the Chilterns, I felt myself equipped to begin work. I had, of course, to check random recollections, to see that remembered villages had not suffered a road-widening or that inns first visited years ago had not acquired a new and often spurious antiquity....

Scarcely could I have deceived myself more. It was not that memory misled me or that the last few years have brought many changes; it was, rather, that my acquaintance had been at best selective, too often superficial. Time and again when following ways that had long seemed familiar and revisiting places I thought I knew well, I have been surprised—at times almost shocked—to realise how much I had formerly overlooked, how much more there was to see, to understand, than had caught the passing glance. Even now I am sure that there is much more than I have been able to tell of, even with the help of family, friends, publishers and local (and very tolerant) residents. I must hope to have included sufficient to persuade the reader to look for more for himself; and if he thinks—as I did—that he already knows the Chilterns he may be in for many pleasant surprises.

ONE

The Icknield Approach

Anyone who has travelled to London from any point between the west and the north will, unless his eyes were undeviatingly fixed on the road ahead, have seen the Chilterns. They rise abruptly out of the low-lying clay plain that stretches from south of the Fens across the Middle Thames. For a length of approaching sixty miles they achieve an escarpment which is in places so steep that only grass and scant thorn bushes can cling to it. A substantial barrier the Chilterns look, and unmistakably chalk in their smooth swelling and in the whiteness that shows through on the steeper slopes and at the upper rim of the fields below them where the plough has bitten above the fertile fringe of the plain.

To travellers from London making for the North, the Midlands or Wales, the Chilterns appear less dramatic. The long slope south-eastwards is more gentle and the chalk has been worn into a hundred valleys, most of them apparently dry, up which roads can climb more leisurely. The Chilterns there appear rather as ridges running parallel with the road and capped often with beechwoods, though now and again a lesser side-valley—a 'bottom' as it is called locally—opens the way for a lane to wind to a farm or a hamlet in the folding hills. It is indeed possible to drive along one or other of the main roads—from Amersham to Wendover, say, or along Watling Street to Dunstable—scarcely aware that the land is rising until on either hand the escarpment of Chiltern opens a way through, and stretching below is the clay plain patchworked with a hundred fields.

These through ways known to a multitude of travellers during the past two thousand years are, however, the newer Chiltern routes. They were brought into use for access to the lower Thames and, later, by the magnet of London. Then the escarpment became a barrier to be pierced. Earlier, when travellers trod the beginnings of the Chiltern routes, they followed the escarpment rather than

the valleys. For them the gaps were obstacles, marshy hollows round which they had to find a way before resuming their path along the line of the escarpment.

The route they trod is among the oldest in Britain. It is the Icknield Way, a name so ancient that the Place-Name Society does not venture an explanation of its origin or meaning—though a visitor can assume the popular derivation from the Iceni who peopled East Anglia at the time of the Roman Conquest and even, if his imagination is up to it, visualise their Queen Boadicea—more accurately Boudicca—driving a chariot along the Way in the manner of the statue on London's Victoria Embankment. But whether or not that tribe gave its name to the Icknield Way, it was already ancient in their day. It formed part of the hill routes that provided a comparatively easy series of ways about a Britain that was over its greater lowland part forest and marsh. It linked the higher land of East Anglia with what is now the Berkshire Ridgeway from which, when the Icknield Way was already old, another hill-way curved southwards to the newly built Stonehenge.

Perhaps because of its sharp-sounding, unassociated name, the Icknield Way has not attained popular interest; or perhaps it is that, sited below the escarpment, it is a little far for family parties from London out for a day's picnic—and there are many attractions in the valleys before the ridge is reached; or perhaps in the first decades of this century when so much of the countryside was cycled, hiked or rambled and then written about, the preliminary journey to Tring or Watlington made a day's trip comparatively expensive; or perhaps it was too near the start of longer trips. Whatever the reason, the name Icknield Way rarely has an immediate appeal. The name of its continuation south of the Thames, the Ridgeway, suggests at once a route that keeps to the crest of the hills and so, in imagination if not always in reality, offers an almost continuous vista of the patchwork of the Vale of the White Horse on one hand and of villages and farms cupped in chalk bottoms on the other. Nor can the name Icknield Way prompt historical, almost romantic, associations like that of the other famous south-country route, the Pilgrims' Way, though we know that in truth that way was, like Icknield, already ancient before medieval pilgrims may (or may not) have journeyed along it. But the Icknield Way remains unassociated, somehow a little unrecognised. Here and there along its sixty miles or more it achieves its name, at least on Ordnance Survey one-inch maps; it even provides at times a street name in

1. The Upper Icknield below Aston Hill

THE ICKNIELD WAYS

2. The Lower Icknield by-passing Aston Rowant

3. View from the top, near Reed

THE CHILTERN CREST

4. View from below, near Ivinghoe

some of the few towns along it. But, except where for a mile west of Tring the Romans incorporated it in their Akeman Street, and for a few stretches where twentieth-century roadmakers have similarly used it, much of it remains a mere by-lane, often for miles little more than a grassy track which we motorists scarcely notice as we cross it to or from London.

It deserves more acknowledgement. In itself the Icknield Way offers one of the best approaches to an understanding of southern England. Merely to travel its length from the neighbourhood of Goring where the Thames forces its curving way through the chalk hills to where the old road from Cambridge climbs over the ridge (and is still marked by the milestones put up in 1725 for the benefit of the stage-coaches), the passer-by would glimpse much of all that has gone to make England. He would—to take a few random examples—pass fields that began to be shaped when the first ploughs were fashioned, villages that started their lives five hundred years before the Norman Conquest, and the first twentieth-century attempt at town-planning; he would pass the church in which John Hampden refused to pay his Ship Money and follow some miles of the route William the Conqueror took while he waited for Saxon London to accept his victory near Hastings as decisive; he would cross canals from the pre-railway age and motorways from the post-railway age; he would see all this and much more before he ended up below the lonely Neolithic barrow on Therfield Heath above Royston.

And if the traveller turned aside now and again, if he made detours up some of the lanes that wind over the ridge and then, more gradually, tilt down to the hamlets and villages in the bottoms, he would find himself in a very different but still undeniably Chiltern landscape—or, rather, a subtly changing series of landscapes. For the range, though continuously chalk, alters considerably in its sixty miles. The northeastern end is a land of smoother hills and wide, almost hedgeless fields that have for a thousand years grown barley for ale to slake Londoners' thirsts. To the southwest are bolder hills and the great beech-woods, vividly blue-carpeted in spring and richly copper in autumn—though perhaps at their loveliest when pale winter sunshine filters through the high tracery of branch and twig and slants on to the silver-grey trunks. By contrast with the open northeastern Chilterns, the southwestern end was, almost into living memory, a secret, seldom visited land, its inhabitants dark of hair and slight of build being—so it

was asserted—descendants of Celtic peoples who had through two thousand years contrived to remain in their hidden valleys. Since then railways and the car have brought newcomers to build— fortunately not too frequently outside the towns—their twentieth-century and often suburban homes or to buy up and refurbish the older houses, and so make the area appear truly English. Yet the name Chiltern, for all its English sound, is Celtic in origin, and here and there place names from pre-Roman times survive. And the whole region must once have had a very different feel about it. Almost the first written mention we have, the phrase of a seventh-century monk, refers not to the woods and farms and fields but to the 'deserts of Chiltern'.

The Icknield Way: so, following custom, I have called the ancient route, but it would be more accurate to refer to the Icknield Ways. For much of its length the route is doubled on the maps: an 'Upper Icknield Way' and a 'Lower Icknield Way' are acknowledged by topographers and archaeologists.

These are, however, the end of a long and complex history, the products in part of the needs of Iron-Age rulers, Roman engineers, medieval merchants and cattle-drovers, later enclosure commissioners and, finally, twentieth-century road-builders satisfying motorists' needs. The Icknield Way certainly did not begin life as the road or bridlepath or green lane we now see. When for reasons of geology—which we shall have to consider in a little more detail shortly—the first Neolithic herdsman found the mile-wide strip of land along the foot of the Chiltern escarpment suited to their rudimentary husbandry, they did not tread a single or even a double clearly defined Way. (If they had done so the subsequent multitudes of users would have worn a narrow, deeply sunken track, and Icknield is never that.) In the beginnings of Icknield the idea of set fields and defined routes was far ahead. The naturally thinly covered escarpment that could be used as grazing ground, with here and there a random clearing which could for a few seasons raise a crop of grain, would have had to provide for the Neolithic families; and they must every few seasons have moved on when their local soil became exhausted. So Icknield was then not a single or double track but an intertwining of many paths following the comparatively bare escarpment. Not until more permanent and defined settlement became a possibility and a necessity would have begun the process of confining Icknield to two or three ways, one following the foot of the escarpment (approximating to our 'Upper Icknield') and

4

another (our 'Lower Icknield') roughly along the edge of the clay which into early medieval times was too heavy, too wet and too forested to encourage agriculture.

Nowadays the Upper Icknield is assumed to have been the earlier defined, the Lower one 'more recent'. This assumption rests largely on the fact that the Lower Icknield was at least in part used by the Romans. The most detailed work to date—*Roman Roads in the South-east Midlands*, by the group of archaeologists known collectively as the 'Viatores'—implies that much of the Lower Icknield is Roman in origin, and certainly its straighter stretches appear to have been, in Roman engineering fashion, aligned on distant points. But many Roman roads are known to have utilised earlier trackways; and the continuation of the Lower Icknield beyond the known Roman limits (and often linking known earlier sites) suggests an early doubling.

This doubling of ancient hill-routes is by no means uncommon. For much of its length the Berkshire Ridgeway has, just at the foot of its chalk escarpment, a more or less parallel route that was old enough to have been used but not straightened by the Romans. The nameless route which for a dozen miles west of Lewes uses the ridge of the Sussex Downs has similarly a lane following the line between the chalk and the fields which stretch out to the North. The famous Pilgrims' Way, which runs below the escarpment of the North Downs, is doubled for much of its length by a way keeping to the crest. Indeed this doubling is so frequent that it gave rise, some years ago, to the theory that the weather had caused travellers to tread alternative paths, the upper one during the winter when the lower one was likely to be impassable from flooding and the lower one during the drier months. To anyone who has read of medieval road conditions when a traveller—and in at least one instance his horse, too—might be drowned in a water-filled hole on the king's highway such a theory does not seem improbable.

Unlike most other doubled hill-routes, however, both the Icknield Ways run below the escarpment—at least according to the maps. The possibility of another route following the crest is not topographically recognised; but some archaeologists are not so sure. Though much of the southern half of the Chilterns was thickly forested and therefore—so it is sometimes asserted—likely to have discouraged travellers from venturing along the ridge, there are hints that the woods we now enjoy may give an impression of greater, more hindering woodland than nature provided. And there is a

continuous line of by-roads and footpaths from the Thames about Whitchurch at least as far as the Princes Risborough gap which some archaeologists believe preserves the memory of a continuation of Berkshire's Ridgeway northwards. Only more archaeology, enlightened perhaps by as yet undiscovered 'finds', can confirm or deny the suggestion of this third Icknield Way; and whether or not this crest-keeping route is ancient, it certainly provides at times a delightful alternative to the topographically correct Icknield approach.

It is these alternative Icknield Ways—the two certainties, the third only as yet a possibility—that give the Icknield approach its appeal. They provide variety to suit whatever means of travelling is chosen: for, except for a few brief stretches—and those are mostly the approaches to the towns—one Icknield is sure to be a metalled road while another is a green lane or a footpath. And if the traveller is not rigidly determined to follow the cartographers' or the 'Viatores'' interpretations, if he is open-minded enough to hope that at least some of the linking lanes and footpaths remember variations of the primitive Way, he can follow the Icknield approach by car, by cycle, on foot or if he—or more likely these days she—is so inclined, on horseback.

Perhaps such a statement needs reassurance; so here is a brief summary (which can be followed easily on the O.S. one-inch maps):

Taking Goring as the Thames crossing from the Ridgeway, the first two miles of the Icknield Way is a minor road running northeastwards (though a track halfway along it leading up to Woodcote provides a way to the ridge sequences with their beechwoods). The first stretch to be named begins a hundred yards north of Icknield Farm as a footpath soon to become a grass track heading across country past Ipsden and then, as a minor road, to approach Ewelme. A mile short of that village the road divides; it is from here that the Upper and Lower Icknield appear to separate. The road that passes through Ewelme becomes B 4009 to Watlington after which, as a path, it skirts Shirburn and Lewknor to achieve a name as the Lower Icknield Way. The other fork south of Ewelme rises leisurely and at the foot of Sliding Hill (and what that name might suggest!) gains recognition as the Upper Icknield Way. From there for nearly a dozen miles until Princes Risborough comes in sight, it is a wide bridle path, and for much of that time it is accompanied by a ridge-top

lane from Nettlebed to the Oxford Road, from which a series of footpaths leads until below Wain Hill the route joins the Upper Icknield a mile and a half from Princes Risborough.

From about a mile north of Risborough the Lower Icknield Way continues as B 4009 heading for Tring. The Upper one as a path skirts south of Risborough to go across the fields to the village of Whiteleaf after which it, too, becomes a road; but from Whiteleaf, if the traveller prefers to walk and accepts the possibility of the third, ridge-following Icknield, a footpath leads up into the beechwoods to make its way round the Iron Age fort on Pulpit Hill, crosses the hollow in which Chequers lies and then climbs along the ridge of Coombe Hill to meet the metalled Upper Icknield a quarter-mile from Wendover station (and on the way the traveller can, if his political views suggest the necessity, literally look down on the Prime Minister if he should be in his official country residence).

From Wendover to Tring, where the Upper Icknield has become the A 4011 and the Lower a minor road, it is similarly possible to follow footpaths that lead from the Iron Age fort on Boddington Hill to where a choice of paths lead down to Tring. (An alternative and less strenuous way for the walker is to find the beginning of the old Wendover canal and to follow its winding towpath to the hamlet of Bulbourne where it is crossed by the Upper Icknield—a possibility about which more will be said later.)

Three miles northeast of Tring, just beyond Ivinghoe, the two official Icknield Ways join to become the B 489 to Dunstable —that is, they join according to the map. To do so the Lower Icknield has to make an improbable turn in Ivinghoe village, and just at that point a lane leads off to become within half a mile a footpath heading for Edlesborough church on its ancient mound —just the line that the Lower Icknield, had it persisted in the course it has followed for a dozen miles, would have taken. And after passing 'Maiden Bower', an Iron Age fort a mile out of Dunstable, this lower, unnamed route can be followed until north of Luton it links up with the recognised Icknield Way. Meanwhile, the named Icknield Way following the line of the upper one has after passing below Ivinghoe Beacon become the B 489 to Dunstable, then the A 505 to the outskirts of Luton.

The road from Luton to Hitchin and on to Baldock may not be as ancient as Icknield; but it was certainly in use early in

Saxon times and it offers fine views over a countryside which, though still undeniably Chiltern, is opening out and hinting of the wide sweeps ahead. The Icknield Way, now singular and continuing the line of the Lower one, remains by contrast a little frequented green lane for ten miles except for where a cross-country lane uses it briefly and another quarter-mile as part of Ickleford's street. After another rural mile, at the ancient earthwork of Wilbury, it takes a more easterly direction to become the main street of Letchworth and so on to Baldock where it merges into the road from Luton. But a couple of miles farther on the Icknield Way (so named), the A 505, has acquired a lower parallel route, a green track known for seven miles as Ashwell Street. It looks as if between Wilbury, three miles west of Baldock, and the village of Ashwell, three miles northeast of Baldock, the Lower Icknield has made its way unrecognised along lanes and footpaths.

For a mile and a half east of Royston a single Icknield continues the A 505 until that road bears off northeast. There the Way continues more easterly, a track for three gently undulating miles below that extension of the Chilterns usually with some exaggeration called the East Anglian Heights. As the valley of the Bourne, a tributary of the Cam, comes into view, the Way becomes less assured. Lanes lead down to probable river-crossings but hereabouts it is difficult to be certain; even the course of the Roman road which carved a line from Great Chesterford to the Roman town near Braughing is barely traceable among the bouncing hills. Beyond the Bourne the Icknield Way loses its identity though by-roads and paths, often seeming to have little purpose in themselves, maintain its direction intermittently, and here and there on older maps of Suffolk they are accorded the name.

Such, in brief summary, are the Icknield Ways, varying between roads which, often following the 'spring line' of the hills, give wide views over the vale, and tracks ambling leisurely through ancient farmlands or striding along the Chiltern crest. Merely to follow one or other, using whatever means of travelling is convenient, is worthwhile at any season. To watch from a car (from a passenger seat preferably) the seeming endless sequence of bold thrust and rounded withdrawal of the chalk escarpment, to view more distantly the impressive line of the wood-capped hills, to catch sight through the beech-trunks along the crest route of a hamlet and its fields

cupped in an almost sheer-sided combe—these delights the Icknield Ways offer to every traveller. But they are only a fraction of
all that is to be seen, to be experienced, by way of the Icknield
approach.

As has already been mentioned, the Icknield Ways originally
followed the strip of land along the foot of the Chiltern escarpment.
Geology had made it more fertile than the thin-grassed slopes and
more readily cultivable than the heavy clay to the north; it was
also well supplied with springs. So along that strip the Neolithic
farmers made their settlements, the Iron-Agers and the Romans
built their dwellings and later the Saxons began the villages that
still stand there. Meanwhile the valleys and bottoms within the
hills were being penetrated and so, rather later than the settlements
below the escarpment, the land there began to be worked. Still
later as trade developed and travelling became easier towns grew up
at nodal points. All these—the villages and towns along the Ways
and those over the ridge and linked to them by steep lanes—bring
humanity to the varied landscape. They are man in a setting that
is at once ancient and twentieth century. They tell collectively of
man's activities, of his work and hopes, of his generosity and his
desire for gain, of his fears and his beliefs, through a thousand years
and more. Every one of them has something to tell of what man
has been and is—if the traveller can see it.

That is, of course, the essence of travelling—not so much what
is to be seen as what the traveller sees in it. To gain some understanding it is necessary to have some framework of knowledge; but
merely to know that an historical somebody lived in such-and-such
a house or that the former inhabitants of such-and-such a place
witnessed an event is only a starting-point.

It is the purpose of this book to provide some of those starting-
points, to draw the traveller's attention to something of what has
been and what is; from then on, his understanding must take over.
To say all that might be said of the region would be unwieldy—and
presumptuous, for appreciation is a personal matter.

To maintain some order in what could easily become a meandering and formless record of impressions, the region is in the following
chapters divided into man-made sections, each approached from
a stretch of the Icknield Ways and bounded by main roads that
lead through gaps in the ridge—which, incidentally, will provide
motorists with a series of roughly two-sided routes beginning and
ending on a convenient main road. It will also provide them with

alternatives to the much-used main roads if, when travelling to or from London, they have time for a more leisurely and often more attractive way. Some indications are given of how—by car or on foot—much of what is to be found in each section can be reached. But these are mere incidentals. It is what the traveller makes of them that matters.

TWO

The Making of the Chilterns

As everyone who in a school geography book glimpsed a diagram of the London Basin will know, the Chilterns are the northern rim of the great slab of chalk that underlies the valley of the Lower Thames. At some incomprehensibly remote time the chalk slab was level; but before life had progressed far beyond the age of the humblest of sea creatures that slab had suffered a wide variety of upheavals, immersions and inundations, and all climates from the tropical to the arctic.

To attempt to describe in detail the geological make-up of the Chilterns is beyond the purpose of this book—which statement is more than face-saving, as anyone who has worked his way through such a book as Wooldridge and Linton's *Structure, Surface and Drainage in South-east England* will know; there are few more geologically complex areas. Fortunately we are concerned not so much with what is under the soil as with the surface itself and what man has made of it. After all, man has for over fifty thousand years contrived to win his livelihood from that surface. It is only during the last century or so that he has become concerned about the 'Palaeozoic Floor' several hundred feet under his hunting ground and the 'Pre-Tertiary Movements' which may, or may not, have assisted his husbandry.

Here we shall content ourselves with digging—metaphorically— only slightly into the geological past. And first, a deepish look at what is under the chalk: a layer of greensand (which can appear more brownish than green) and then a thicker layer of gault, a stiff, heavy, impervious clay. This must be our starting-point, for that non-porous gault traps the rainwater that filters through the porous chalk. This fact has modified man's activities in the Chiltern area, for the gault has provided a natural underground reservoir in a land that would be otherwise almost waterless. Springs issuing naturally from under the chalk—where the water trapped

11

by the gault has to overflow—have provided a first necessity for life, notably along the Icknield Way. Later, when man had learnt the art of well-digging, he could add to those natural sources by tapping the 'underground reservoir' vertically.

The chalk, like the greensand and gault on which it rests, was laid down by water, and originally over a much larger area than it now occupies. The often-repeated statement that chalk is composed of shells of microscopic sea-creatures is an exaggeration. It is composed much more of 'exceedingly fine calcareous matter', to quote the Regional Geological Survey, 'probably produced organically from the disintegration of planktonic algae'. At least three layers of chalk are recognisable, suggesting three periods of its composition separated by periods when the chalk was raised above the contemporary sea-level. During these times of emergence, and continuing into more recent times, the flints associated with the chalk were formed. These are composed of silica found in the chalk. Being partially soluble in water, the silica as it was washed down in the chalk gathered into globules which ultimately solidified again.

Contributing much more to the present appearance of the Chilterns is what happened after the chalk was laid down. Times of uplift caused some buckling of the chalk slab and began its marked hollowing towards the centre (though the Thames valley was still millions of years and many disturbances away). At a period of prolonged but partial subsidence, the sea spread across the northern and presumably lower stretches of chalk and began the process of wearing away much of the slab, gradually shaping a cliff-line which approximates to the escarpment.

The rain of this period and of subsequent times changed the surface chalk. Rainwater, possibly at times slightly acid from the electrolytic effect of lightning, chemically attacked the chalk, producing a more clay-like substance to which wind-blown dust, sand and decaying vegetable matter would have adhered, but leaving the flints untouched. The resultant 'clay-with-flints', to use the geologists' term, formed a capping to the hill-tops and ridges which later would support forests. Often unexpectedly acid, the clay-with-flints varies in depth from a few inches to approaching fifty feet. It also varies in quality, sometimes being heavy and difficult to cultivate, often producing workable loam particularly when chalk has been reintroduced.

Long before this capping of clay-with-flints was near completion, the chalk tilted eastwards and into what we can now begin to

think of as the future London Basin water intruded for long periods. Water can build up as well as wash away, and successive inundations left deposits mainly of clays (the London clay was one) which were during periods of uplift in part worn down by wind and weather. The remainders of these deposits account for what appears to a newcomer to the Chilterns a surprising peculiarity where on a ridge expected to be continuously chalk ploughing reveals soils that are clearly clayey.

By the time these deposits were laid down the outline of the Chiltern region was becoming recognisable. But still there were to come the Ice Ages to sculpture the land nearer to its present shape, particularly the Third Ice Age when the greater part of Britain was covered by a huge ice-sheet and the whole of it suffered arctic conditions. The effects of this Ice Age produced the marked difference between the eastern Chilterns and the western. The ice-sheet, working its way southward, was checked by the chalk escarpment to the west; to the east the ice was forced over the ridge and its most southerly lobes reached almost to the site of London. The escarpment above Watlington and Wendover has been left steep and clear; the ridge above Royston and Baldock has been in part ground down, bevelled into lower, gentler contours.

The ice-sheet was in effect a huge glacier moving imperceptibly but persistently, and by its immense weight grinding and tearing the land over which it moved. Rocks and soils were dragged along by the ice, often for great distances. Prominent among these rocks are the 'brick-earth' and the 'boulder clay' of the geologists, brought by the ice from further north. Originally these clays were heavy, hard to drain and not readily cultivable; but the ice-sheet, dragging them over the eastern Chilterns, also caught up chalk; and the mixing was agriculturally beneficial. It produced over the eastern Chilterns stretches of workable loam, much of it capable of growing the barley that has for centuries made Ware the centre of the malting industry.

The eventual melting of the ice caused other changes to the landscape. The immense amount of water gradually freed must have swollen the rivers and so widened and deepened the valleys—many of the presently dry bottoms were then watercourses—along which were left gravelly, sandy or pebbly deposits, adding yet more types of surface rock to the already complex pattern.

Each Ice Age was followed by an interglacial period of near-tropical temperatures when dense jungle spread over the lower

ground. Fauna appropriate to such conditions thrived—and at some as yet undetermined time the earlier types of Palaeolithic man appeared.

He left his traces in the Chiltern region as elsewhere. But whether the being who made the first crude flint tools—the roughly shaped 'core tools' or eoliths of the archaeologists—was our direct ancestor or not can be left to the anthropologists; the illustrations, based on surmise and imagination, that in childhood were our introduction to remote prehistory may make us hope not. Not for many thousands of years, not until the warmer interval between the third and the last Ice Age, did the being whom we hopefully or conceitedly name *homo sapiens* tread Britain and leave behind his finer tools fashioned skilfully not from the cores of flints but from sharp fragments struck from them. The clear craftsmanship when contrasted with the earlier crudeness enables us to acknowledge a one-ness with him.

It is assumed that early man came to Britain from Europe, crossing what was left of the chalk ridge that still linked Britain to France, and spread northwards as the ice melted and the animals on which he preyed moved into the vegetation that gradually claimed the empty land. The Chiltern region, when at last we can begin to visualise man in it, seems to have been a soggier and cruder place than it is today. Forests covered the hills, large swamps sprawled over the lowlands. If the somewhat random collection of 'finds', mainly hunting tools, is an accurate guide, early man appears to have tried to avoid both forest and marsh by living mainly on the gravel 'river terraces'.

Palaeolithic man made no impression on the landscape. The hunter has no incentive to modify his habitat. The most that early man must have done was to erect rough shelters of branch and mud, for chalk forms no natural caves. And we must suppose that these Old Stone-agers were satisfied with the flints they found on the surface for their tools; the flint mines discovered on Peppard Common and elsewhere were of a later date.

Not until Neolithic times, a mere 6,000 or so years ago, did man begin, at first very tentatively, to use and modify his Chiltern environment. With the twin discoveries of cattle-rearing and crop-growing the restricting habitat-accepting way of the hunter could be, and ultimately had to be, modified. But the process was probably a long-drawn-out one.

As has already been mentioned, it was with the arrival of these

New Stone-agers that the strip of comparatively cultivable land below the Chiltern escarpment, the Icknield strip, began to have its peculiar virtues recognised. It is, geologically speaking, a complex area, the shore of ancient seas on which glacial deposits were left as the ice-sheet of the Third Ice Age melted, modified by meltwater and the later chalky downwash from the escarpment—all contriving to produce a soil more readily workable than the clay stretching alongside it. But at the time the New Stone-agers took their first steps along the Icknield route, the strip must still have been largely forested. It must have been the accessibility which first drew them: the lowest few feet of the escarpment levelling out from the steep slope above and clear of the forest growth provided the only continuously open land route in the large area between the North Downs and the limestone belt of the Midlands.

The incipient Icknield Way provided more. The scanty covering of the escarpment was grazing for sheep and goats, not much by later standards but more available than much that forested and marshy prehistoric Britain could provide. And probably within the varied soils of the Icknield strip were patches of less dense vegetation, glades where cattle could find some nourishment. And, as has been mentioned, it is along this first Icknield route where chalk meets gault that springs issue. The three together made permanent settlement possible.

To us, imagining ourselves grasping a flint-edged axe to fell an oak or seizing an 'antler-pick' to dig up a troublesome tree-root, the clearing of primeval forest appears a formidable task. Neolithic farmers may have had an aid that we overlook. Certainly the Anglo-Saxons, faced 5,000 years later with a comparable problem, used fire—and they had superior iron tools and slaves to help them. Once a stretch had been partly cleared by burning, the tribal pigs and goats could be relied upon to resist a return of the forest. A full thousand years before Neolithic farmers appeared in Britain both animals had been domesticated in the Middle East—from where the New Stone-agers had indirectly acquired the rudiments of their husbandry; and both animals are omnivorous, ready to eat up the weeds and saplings that might threaten to reclaim fire-cleared land.

The Neolithic techniques, though full of promise, were as yet merely beginnings. Only in very favourable circumstances could men have relied on their farming skills for their livelihood. Far more often the food from their patches of crop-land and their

herds must have been supplemented by hunting; or perhaps it was the other way round, as is shown by the recent excavations at the Neolithic site of Waulud's Bank near Luton: 'Finds of many arrowheads and the closeness of the marshes [about the upper Lea] suggest a hunting economy supplemented by animal husbandry and agriculture.' The transition from hunter to farmer must have been a far more protracted process than the successive chapters of our school textbooks implied.

Judging from the more random finds—and if the visitor wishes to behold them he must visit a local museum—the Neolithic peoples in the Chiltern region were rather more adventurous than their predecessors. Their polished flint tools have been found not only along the Icknield strip but also in the valleys and bottoms within the hills. They settled the sandy ridge of Lodge Hill, a mile along the Risborough gap (as did later both Bronze Age and Iron Age people); a habitation site has been discovered near High Wycombe, and the flint-mines known as Peppard Common, Pitstone, and near High Wycombe, hint of the beginnings of a manufacturing industry.

How much of the New Stone-agers' agricultural efforts were taken over by their successors and so can be regarded as the beginnings of later areas of cultivation it is impossible to say. Their Icknield route has survived, together with some of their first modifications of the landscape. Of these Waulud's Bank has already been mentioned, to which one day may be added something of another earthwork, 'Maiden Bower' above Dunstable, though as it now appears, its Neolithic beginnings have been overlaid by an Iron Age fort. Perhaps other similar earthworks, now ascribed to the Iron Age, will be found to have had Neolithic origins, for their herds and their dwellings must have needed some protection. But their most significant additions to the landscape were their long barrows. Six have been identified in the Chiltern area though only that on Therfield Heath remains complete enough to give some impression of their handiwork. Probably the burial mound of a tribal chief, it has tenuous links with the religions of the Middle East, though in their travels through distance and time the religious beliefs and practices have remained simple, achieving masterpieces at Avebury and Stonehenge but never so far afield as remote Britain attaining the magnificence of pyramid or ziggurat.

It is no longer possible to classify the successors of the New Stone-agers conveniently into Bronze-agers and Iron-agers as though the new metallic discoveries abruptly ended one period and began the

next. It has become increasingly clear that during the two millennia preceding the Roman Conquest, Britain was subjected to two series of new arrivals, the first using bronze in improving weaponry and tools, the later knowing iron ... to which may be added distinctions in pottery and changes in burial customs. It is still uncertain whether these newcomers were intent on colonisation or whether the various waves of invaders were a comparative few who, being better armed and more war-like than the people they found, were able to set up what we would call military dictatorships. Archaeologists can distinguish, mainly from potsherds and burial habits, several distinct Bronze Age peoples, though their relations with the Neolithic survivors (who may well have continued their business of food production much as usual under new overlords) are still far from clear.

As to the Bronze-agers' contribution to the Chiltern countryside we can be a little more certain. We owe to them most, but not all, of the round barrows that stand in prominent places along the crest. Such burial mounds, in which the ashes of a cremation contained in an earthenware pot (usually long ago deposited in a museum) are far more frequent than inhumation, may have stretched the whole length of the Chilterns; their absence northeastwards of Luton is probably due to the plough having levelled the mound. At some points, such as about the Risborough gap, on the hills above Ivinghoe, and above Dunstable, a cluster of round barrows (some of which were used for later interments) imply comparatively densely populated areas. Some finds of the period, such as the bronze sword from Hawridge near Chesham and the bronze axe from Hazlemere near High Wycombe, suggest that they intruded more into the upland areas than their predecessors had done.

To the Iron-Agers we owe most of the so-called forts along the defensible crest of the Chilterns and also some sited in less obviously military places, such as that at Cholesbury near Chesham. That so many are above the Icknield strip underlines the continuing importance of that readily cultivable area. But if these forts served as refuges in times of emergency they were a long, uphill way to drive the tribal herds from settlements beyond the foot of the escarpment; their siting implies that the natural cover along the crest had been sufficiently reduced to provide grazing. Certainly the last wave of Iron Age people, the Belgic tribes who arrived during the last century B.C., had cleared extensive areas for cultivation both in the Hitchin–Baldock neighbourhood and further south about

their settlements—probably crude towns—near St Albans, Welwyn and Braughing. Indeed one Belgic people, the Catuvellauni, had acquired a kingdom stretching across much of the southern Chilterns with its capital at Wheathampstead, which in 54 B.C. Julius Caesar is believed to have captured. After his departure the Catuvellauni constructed a new capital at Prae Wood near the future Verulamium (St Albans) from which for forty years before the Roman Conquest a Belgic king Cunobelin ruled a kingdom which reached from the Essex coast to beyond the Chiltern crest.

Besides the forts and some known Iron-Age habitation sites there are about the Chilterns other banks and ditches, some probably connected with Iron-Age tribal defences; there is also that meandering but persistent bank-and-ditch, Grim's Dyke, which crops up to the southeast of the escarpment and elsewhere. Some authorities tentatively classify this as Iron Age and others, also tentatively, as Anglo-Saxon. Such uncertainty, giving the rather lowly ancient monument a touch of mystery, will have to be investigated at viewing time. Meanwhile there is the Roman contribution to note.

That the Romans left their mark on the Chiltern region needs no emphasising. Three of their most military roads, Ermine Street, Watling Street and Akeman Street, now being demoted by motorways, have for eighteen hundred years served the country at large and the inhabitants of the Chilterns incidentally. In addition the Romans used, metalling sometimes and apparently sometimes leaving as little more than tidied-up tracks, a number of lesser roads (which may have been in use before their arrival); among these, as has been mentioned, are lengths of the Icknield Ways. Some of these lesser roads disappeared during early medieval times and have only recently been traced by the indefatigable 'Viatores', who tell about all that is known to date.

Significantly Roman activity, both in road construction and in building generally, is much more prominent in the eastern half of the Chilterns. There is no known Roman road in the large area between Akeman Street, using the Tring gap, and the Thames—with the possible exception of the Lower Icknield Way between Aston Clinton and Watlington after which, according to the 'Viatores', it peters out, implying that it was little more than a local by-road. Such an absence of roads would prompt the assumption that the Romans ignored the southern Chilterns; but the known dwelling-sites of the period—sometimes villas, sometimes 'unidentified buildings'—at such places as Bix high up beside the present

5. *Therfield Heath, near Royston*

CHILTERN COUNTRY

6. *Farm in the hills, near West Wycombe*

7. *Bassingbourn, near the Lower Icknield*

CHILTERN VILLAGES

8. *Aldbury, under the hills*

Wallingford–Henley road, and Hughenden tucked away in a valley above High Wycombe, suggest that at least the more accessible parts of the area were settled, perhaps being reached along tracks that have been buried under the later lanes.

More easterly along the Chilterns, as we would expect, the pattern of settlement becomes more widespread, though there are still quite large areas where as yet little trace of Roman intrusion has been reported. When the known habitation sites are plotted on the map, one gets the impression that even in this more cultivable part of the Chilterns settlement was a somewhat patchy process, comparable to the picture often imagined of medieval England with the villages and their lands appearing like islands of cultivation in a sea of forest, only rather more so for, unless many a village has yet to discover its Roman origin, medieval settlement was much more thorough.

For those who wish to see the actual Roman finds, visits to local museums are essential. But for the traveller there are glimpses beyond the roads (which always look more impressively Roman on the map or in an air-photograph than they do on the ground). Here and there Roman bricks may be seen in the fabric of an ancient church, indicating that a Roman building, perhaps as yet undiscovered, stood nearby. But the brick must be Roman: thin, reddish and professionally baked. The belief that the art of brick-making was lost between the departure of the legions and late medieval times has been shown to be inaccurate. A brick-like fragment in a church wall may not be Roman but the coarser, often crudely fashioned and ill-baked attempt of a Saxon brickmaker—though, in truth, a Saxon brick among the flints would be more of a rarity and, perhaps, more to muse about.

Of the three Roman towns in the Chiltern region—Dunstable, Braughing and Letchworth—more will be said when they are visited. In the meantime, by way of a pointer to the changes of Roman times in this (for them) comparatively insignificant part of the country, it may be of interest to note how recent excavation has illustrated the pattern of economic and social change long suspected by critics of Roman Britain.

Once it was possible to believe that Roman Britain had enjoyed the civilising influence of the Pax Romana unclouded until the fateful A.D. 410 when, the Legions having been called to protect Rome itself, hordes of savage Angles and Saxons and Jutes wantonly massacred the helpless and civilisation-softened Britons, and brought

in the Dark Ages. Recent careful excavation has both dispelled some of the darkness of the Dark Ages and shown up the Glory that was Rome as tarnished and, at times, almost tawdry. There is no doubt that even in the more pacific and prosperous southeast there were at times slumps and recessions on a comparatively large scale—to which were added, during the last century of Roman Britain, insecurity as a result of a prolonged invasion from the North and increasing attacks by Germanic raiders. Disorder on such a scale made life in the countryside increasingly unsafe and caused villas and farms to be abandoned while persisting unemployment caused deterioration in town-life. Archaeologists have found many instances of buildings, even important municipal ones, falling into ruin or being left to decay long before the Legions departed.

The decay of Verulamium has long been known. The recent excavations at Braughing, apparently a locally important town, confirm the general pattern of decline, as is shown by the summary in the H.M.S.O. Report for 1971:

> Excavations … established a wide range of occupation with pottery and coins from early and mid-First century A.D. to the end of the Fourth century A.D. The main structural evidence, all of it timber buildings, belongs to the first two centuries A.D. … In the Third century the area seems to have been turned into a dump and garden area…. By at the latest A.D. 400 occupation had ceased and the Roman levels were overlaid by a thick layer of silt formed by the slow-moving stream.

Braughing appears to have decayed a full half-century before the Angles and Saxons appeared.

The Anglo-Saxon takeover of the Chiltern region appears to have been, as in many other parts of Britain, a piecemeal affair. The two recorded items from adjoining territory offer little guidance: in A.D. 429 St Germanus met religious leaders apparently somewhere north of Verulamium and witnessed a British victory; under A.D. 571 the Anglo-Saxon Chronicle tells of the men of Wessex defeating Britons at the unidentified 'Bedcanford' and so winning the towns of Benson, Limbury near Luton, Aylesbury and Eynsham. This is held to imply that a British state of some kind survived in this area until then. For hints of what may have been happening elsewhere in the Chiltern region we have to look at the place-names.

It is now over thirty years since Collingwood and Myres in their

Roman Britain and English Settlements drew attention to the significance of place-names ending in 'ing' or 'ingas'; they are among the earliest of Anglo-Saxon names. The 'ing' syllable, usually a suffix to a personal name, denotes 'tribe of' or 'people of' and belongs to the period of Anglo-Saxon settlement before the kingdoms were in being. Such names are usually to be found along the coast—Hastings and Worthing are examples—or like Reading and Goring on navigable rivers.

In the Chiltern region are other early settlements. Hitchin, which remembers the name of the Hicce, an early tribe, suggests that the Icknield Way was, as from Neolithic times, a means of access to inland Britain. Further south are Braughing and Throcking; their appearance on the map so far from an obvious point of entry raises a question about which historians have long disputed.

The names of most towns and villages of England are of Anglo-Saxon origin: the 'hams' and 'tons' and 'burys' that are to be found all over the map to which from the ninth century the Danes added their 'bys' and 'nesses'. (The 'casters' and 'chesters' are of course Anglo-Saxon attempts to say the Latin for 'camp' which they dubbed almost every Roman settlement they found.) This stress on English origins in the early days of place-naming gave the impression that the great majority of the villages and towns were of Saxon or Danish foundation. That some Roman towns had been apparently deserted and that some stretches of Roman road had become overgrown was held to demonstrate Anglo-Saxon indifference to everything British (which they called 'Welsh', meaning 'foreign'). Probably unintentionally, the early researchers into place-names—who did their work with a thoroughness for which we all should be grateful—left an impression of a very English England in which the Romans had left a few remains but to which the Britons, Romanised or not, had contributed little more than an occasional river- or hill-name.

Increasingly during the past decade or two that impression has been challenged. It would be hazardous for a non-expert to take sides in what might be called the 'continuity controversy', but it does seem a little improbable that Anglo-Saxon invaders, intent on setting up their homes in the country, would have ignored what was there for them to use. It is almost as if we are expected to assume that the tribal leaders, after winning an area, ordered their men to turn their backs on those parts of it which had been brought under cultivation in order to set about the laborious business of

clearing forest and draining marsh. Surely where Anglo-Saxon would-be settlers found land which was still being worked or had been abandoned so recently that only a few years' forest growth had begun to reclaim it, they would have seized it rather than tackle land which had never been tamed? And would not they, having won their land, name it after themselves rather than struggle to pronounce whatever the Britons they contacted (and probably made slaves) called the place?

Which brings us, perhaps, to a leader named Breah and his people, the 'Breahingas', the 'Braughings' to us. Perhaps accompanied by other tribes who left their names to Throcking and Buntingford they could have approached the neighbourhood of today's Braughing along a Roman road: westwards along Stane Street or more probably southwards along Ermine Street from the Icknield route. And about a mile south of modern Braughing they must have found a Roman town. Its name has been lost and archaeologists are at present trying to discover what the town had been like. Perhaps one day they will learn whether at the time Breah and his tribesmen appeared it was already little more than the shadow of a town from which its few squatters fled or whether the Breahingas had to take it by force. Either way it seems to have been unable to prevent Breah and his tribe from building their settlement on what must have once been part of the town fields.

The five centuries of Anglo-Saxon and, later, Anglo-Danish England must have been a time of gradual development and, in the Chilterns, of gradual penetration into areas not previously settled. Increasingly from the Conversion onwards, law-codes, wills and charters tell indirectly of more land being brought under cultivation, of markets being established by royal command to deal with the increasing trade, and of mints being set up to provide the necessary coin; but the best summary of the period is the Domesday Book. Its system of recording the value and appurtenances of each manor, and sometimes the number of workers and their duties, both at the time it was compiled, in 1086/7, and on the day on which 'King Edward (the Confessor) was alive and dead', 5 January 1066, provides an account both of the effect of twenty years of Norman rule and of the state of much of the country immediately prior to the Conquest. Merely to map the places mentioned—the manors which were often but not invariably the villages and towns—shows that during the 600 years between the disintegration of Roman Britain and the Battle of Hastings a far larger area had been brought

under cultivation than ever before. Though the many settlements recorded would have often been separated from their neighbours by areas which had not yet felt the plough—the wastes of medieval times—and though most villages had commons only partly cleared of their natural cover, every square mile or so had its village or small town, the great majority of which have survived to the present.

The Chiltern region tells on a smaller scale the same story as England as a whole. Though in the more wooded western area flourished the contemporary 'mixed farming'—and it is still that way inclined—the northeastern, more cultivated part had already developed beyond an area of self-supporting villages; for more than a century before the Conquest its farmers had been producing barley and wheat for the London market (London though by our standards still a small city was then already drawing its supplies from a comparatively wide area) and there are hints of other industrial activity. Recent research has been dispelling the impression that later Saxon village life was so self-centred and restricted as was once assumed.

By the time of the Domesday survey there must have been in this northeastern end of the Chilterns, and along the Icknield strip, too, many of those villages which in our early acquaintance with medieval history we tried to draw in our school books: the 'nucleated village' of the archaeologist with its three great open fields divided into strips for sharing and ploughing—though many such villages in fact had only two fields and some came to have four. The gentler landscape to the east and below the escarpment and the more easily worked soils made for such development. Indeed, northeast of Baldock, where the old pattern survived into the present century, the wide, almost hedgeless fields still give an impression of the ancient open cultivation.

In the central and southwestern Chilterns, however, the pattern must from the beginning of Anglo-Saxon settlement have been very different. In the east and along the Icknield strip we can imagine a concerted effort, a whole village turning out to clear the good land little hampered by its gentle contours. In the west the clearing must have been more of a family affair and more limited in scope: small, irregularly shaped patches cleared here and there as the abrupt sweep of a ridge-side or the curve of a bottom determined. And in spite of all that has happened since, the differences are still there to see, and often within a few miles. Take, for example, a lane through Radnage near Stokenchurch and on either hand are the small, variously shaped fields won laboriously from woodland

spreading over sudden ridges and twisting bottoms; climb to the top of the escarpment two miles away and from below Aston Hill stretches a prim patchwork of rectangles of green and brown.

Besides taking over the Anglo-Saxon villages, the Normans made their own contribution to the Chiltern landscape, slighter now in appearance than originally but still appropriately military. To assert the permanence of his triumph at Hastings William the Conqueror, as the Anglo-Saxon Chronicle records, 'wrought castles widely through this country and harassed the miserable people'. Moat-surrounded earthen mottes on which were raised those early castles—initially wooden structures—are still to be found in the Chiltern area. There are at least twenty of them, some with the remains of earthern banks which defended a bailey. Among the earliest are those which were obviously constructed to command the gaps through the Chiltern ridge: Berkhamsted, Little Missenden, Weston Turville near Tring, Saunderton near Princes Risborough, Totternhoe near Dunstable. Others, such as those at Anstey and Benington (a former Saxon royal residence), were baronial foundations; but about others, such as the two at Reed near Royston, we cannot be sure. Such castle sites have often little history and have, as yet, attracted little attention from archaeologists. They may have been among those 'castle works' which the Anglo-Saxon chronicler refers to in the well-known passage telling of the miseries of the 'nineteen long winters' of Stephen's reign:

> When the traitors understood that he [King Stephen] was a mild man, and soft, and good, and no justice executed ... they were all forsworn and forgetful of their troth; for every rich man built his castles, which they held against him.... Then they took those whom they supposed to have any goods, both by night and by day, labouring men and women, and threw them into prison for their gold and silver, and inflicted on them unutterable tortures.... And when the wretched men had no more to give, then they plundered and burned all the towns; that well thou mightest go a whole day's journey and never shouldest thou find a man sitting in a town, nor the land tilled. Then was corn dear, and flesh, and cheese, and butter; for none was there in the land.... To till the ground was to plough the sea; the earth bare no corn, for the land was all laid waste by such deeds; and they said openly that Christ slept, and all his saints.

Only detailed investigation can tell if a particular motte was

among those referred to by the chronicler; but we know that the area between Cambridge and London suffered heavily and that the approaches to Wallingford saw the passage of armies, official and unofficial. The lonelier wastes of the Chilterns would have provided sites for secluded castles for such purposes as the chronicler recorded.

And perhaps people of Stephen's time might have expected the inhabitants at least of the southern Chilterns to be a rather uneasy, lawless lot. Already the office of 'Steward of the Chiltern Hundreds' had come into being to combat the robbing of passers-by. Until well into Stuart times the three hundreds of Desborough (High Wycombe), Burnham and Stoke—and for a while in the thirteenth century another one-and-a-half hundreds comprising the area within the loop of the Thames, too—were considered in need of law-enforcing attention. Not until the mid-seventeenth century had the stewardship of the Chiltern Hundreds become a sinecure and so eventually the means by which a member of the House of Commons, forbidden to sit while enjoying an 'office of profit under the Crown', could in effect resign by being appointed to the position.

Whether by then the inhabitants had become more orderly we do not know. Certainly before and during Stuart times lawlessness of another kind had become apparent throughout much of the Chiltern region. Back in the fourteenth century Wycliffe's Lollards had found many adherents and the Amersham area in particular saw the carrying out of the brutal punishment then customary for heretics. Later John Hampden found among his neighbours in the Wendover area fellow opponents of the Anglican Church of Charles I's time, while a generation later the Quakers became established within the Chiltern Hundreds and further north the Baptists and other 'Independents' were at first secretly and after the Toleration Act of 1689 openly gathering congregations. All told, whether the Chiltern area truly justified the epithet of 'lawless', it seems to have provided many examples of what we would call independence of mind but which for many generations was regarded as 'disobedience' and therefore punishable.

Meanwhile other changes were affecting the Chiltern landscape. The ancient field patterns, the Anglo-Saxon patterns that had become the medieval ones, were being modified. At times of increasing prosperity such as the closing decades of the thirteenth century and, more patchily, from about 1470, when it became profitable to clear more land from the 'wastes', the original villages sprouted hamlets—the 'Mill Ends', 'Northends' and other 'Ends' that dot

the modern map. During such times many comparatively isolated larger houses, surrounded by a moat, were built, perhaps as centres for estates won from former waste, perhaps as the manor-house of a manor which, in order to benefit from the late medieval wool trade, had been turned into a sheep-run. Many of these 'homestead moats', as the archaeologist calls them, are to be found in the Chiltern region; sometimes nearby can be traced unevennesses in the ground which mark the site of former village homes.

From Tudor times onwards the landscape was increasingly changed by enclosure. Only detailed study of a particular parish can determine how and when the ancient common fields, cultivated in many separate strips by their various owners, were transformed to the familiar smaller, hedged fields (of which in theory each former communal owner had his share). For much of the Chilterns as elsewhere enclosure began in random parishes by local agreement; also as elsewhere the process was speeded up from about 1750. By then new farming methods—it was the time of Jethro Tull with his 'horse-hoeing husbandry', of Robert Bakewell's experiments in sheep-breeding, of 'Turnip' Townsend—needed a more individual and compact way of working. The last Chiltern area to retain the old pattern was that around Ashwell and Bygrave, which was not enclosed until the early 1900s.

The Icknield strip and much of the eastern Chilterns were so enclosed, but in the centre and the west, which had known less of the old communal pattern, the change was less marked. The individual nature of its winning from woodland had produced individual farmsteads, their lands, so to speak, 'enclosed' from the beginning. This region was to know more of the enclosure of the village commons, parts of which became in time small-holdings. But when the large area of Berkhamsted Common was threatened with enclosure, so much former common land had disappeared that public feeling turned against the movement (and by then 'common land' had become synonymous in the public mind with land for public use). A long legal battle prevented the enclosing of Berkhamsted Common and enabled the surviving Chiltern commons elsewhere eventually to become public property.

This change in attitude towards enclosure was indirectly brought about by the railways; they had from about 1880 made it possible for more people, particularly Londoners, to know their local countryside, and so added to the demand that public open spaces should be retained. But before the railways the Chiltern region had seen

two other revolutions in transport: the development of the stage-coaches, the result of the road improvements brought haphazardly by the turnpike trusts of the eighteenth century; and the linking of the Thames valley with the canal system which had spread over much of England from the 1780s. Both brought changes, mainly to the little local market-towns which, situated in gaps in the escarpment, thrived on the coach traffic; in many of them can still be seen the inns and cottage-rows and shops, known to us as 'Georgian', built by those who gained from the then-new and then-fast road transport; while along the Grand Junction (now Grand Union) Canal using the Gade-Bulbourne valley, hamlets of 'canal architecture' grew up, cottage-rows for the families of those who worked at wharf and lock, pubs for the passing bargemen, and often in the trim, unpretentious style of the last half of the eighteenth century.

The changes brought by the railways are more widespread and more evident in the rows of brick-walled, slate-roofed houses that sprang up around many a Chiltern town, especially near the stations, and in many a village. (Brick had been in use from Tudor times, but the mass-produced brick and the slate from far afield were spread by the railways.) The development of commuter services such as the old Metropolitan Line to Aylesbury added 'dormitory suburbs' to many of the towns nearer London, a process which the car from the 1920s onwards has increased. Easier road communications had also encouraged the siting of 'light industries' in many towns and so had brought into being newer and often pleasanter suburbs to them. And now there are the motorways.

The effects of these recent developments are various; some recent building blends well with its surroundings, some of it is sited apparently more for the view from its owners' windows than to improve the landscape for the rest of us; some has been clearly the result of thought and discretion, some as clearly for speculative builders' benefit. The balance over the area as a whole is not easy to strike; and condemnation of some individual eyesores should, in fairness, be tempered with the reflection that but for some owners' willingness to take on the costly business of restoration many an old cottage and farmhouse would by now have disappeared. All told, the Chilterns are very much part of the twentieth century.

Though in the foregoing there have been many references to woodland and forested areas, this somewhat specialised subject—

the provider of much delight to the visitor—needs another paragraph or two.

Geologists believe that naturally the whole Chiltern area was heavily wooded. But the woods we now see, especially the hill-top woods of the southwestern half, have been deliberately planted. The dominant beech which thrives on the geological clay-with-flints has been grown for profit certainly since the seventeenth century when, the trees felled young, it provided fuel for London. By the time the increasing use of coal had eaten into this market, beechwood was being used for cheaper furniture. High Wycombe was early associated with the larger pieces while individual craftsmen, known as 'bodgers', used the smaller timber, making it up into stools and chair-legs in huts in the woods. Though the bodgers have gone, there is still a demand for beechwood. Other, more recent woodlands have been planted by the Forestry Commission; these, being partly of quick-growing conifers (to protect young deciduous species), may for a time give a different appearance to their areas. Here and there are patches of common land which, no longer grazed, have been allowed to revert nearly to the wild with a covering often including whitebeam, juniper, thorn, bracken and dogrose.

These changes of the last 300 years may imply that, before then, the Chilterns were not as uniformly wooded as geologists sometimes suggest. Certainly the Domesday references to 'pannage for swine' (acorns and beech-mast) show that there were extensive woods in the lower areas; but elsewhere there are hints that sizeable open spaces usable as rough grazing may have existed naturally. For example, the place-name 'Rotherfield' near Henley, which covers quite a large area often assumed forested, is Anglo-Saxon for 'open land where cattle graze'; and the siting of the Iron Age forts on the crest high above the Icknield strip implies that the tribal herds were near at hand. And the two longest portions of that puzzling earthwork, Grim's Dyke, which may or may not be Iron Age but is certainly ancient, make their way through areas which, if we accept geologists' general impressions, would have been densely wooded—which would, besides adding to the labour of construction, have made the Dyke useless as a defence or a boundary.

Enough of talking about the Chilterns. It is time to take a look at some of the many things they have to show.

THREE

Thames-side

Goring on the Thames is generally recognised as the southern start-ing-point of the Upper Icknield Way. The Way's continuation along the Berkshire Downs, known variously as the Ridgeway, the Port Way, and on some maps as the Icknield Way, starts from Streatley on the opposite bank. Though, as has been mentioned, Icknield must originally have been rather a series of tracks than a single one, a safe crossing-place on so wide an obstacle as the Thames would have tended to make them converge and become temporarily single.

The crossing-place was probably rather below the present Goring bridge. The 'Viatores' suggest a point some three hundred yards downstream 'where a wide green lane leads gently down to the river'. Though they assume a ford at this point to have been in use in Roman times, they have found no evidence of Romanisation of the track which led from it to become, beyond Goring village, the first named length of the Icknield Way. It seems that even the Romans, like the peoples before them and those for a thousand years after them, were content to use the Neolithic route at least for its first ten miles.

We should not, however, leave Goring too hurriedly. Its setting is almost dramatic. Here the Thames has forced its way through the chalk ridge and on both sides the hills, sharply rising and tree-clad, approach so close to the river as to give the impression of restraining it. It is perhaps the most striking length of the whole river, and lovely in spring and autumn when the woods are at their most colourful.

Goring itself is a small, red place, its older streets looking as if they have been hemmed in between hills and river. About the turn of the century red brick 'villas' spread up and down stream and caused many a romantically inclined guidebook of the time to murmur in protest and perhaps prompted Jerome K. Jerome, whose three men visited the place in their boat, to dismiss Goring as

'passing fair enough in its way' though he added that it had the benefit of a railway 'in case you want to slip off without paying your hotel bill'. Since then the trees in the gardens have grown and the way of life the Edwardian houses represented stirs nostalgia. They seem less out of place these days.

Because of its river situation Goring has attracted generations of those who delight in rowing, fishing, punting, motor-boating, or merely looking at or playing in the Thames; and so the village has provided in its inns some welcoming ports of call. The best known, the long, low Miller of Mansfield, owes its name rather unexpectedly to a character in a Midlands ballad—about which the visitor may learn in pleasant surroundings. For those who like their pubs to have a more localised air there are others, such as the Catherine Wheel, up side-streets; and there is the waterside Olde Leather Bottel tucked away along a river-following lane and once called the Water House, not from the Thames but from a nearby spring which was believed to have medicinal virtues. 'Multitudes of people resort to it, and carry the waters away,' a visitor wrote in 1722. 'I am credibly told that there were seven hundred people there last Sunday sennight.' But Goring did not become a Buxton or a Bath. Though long lists of alleged cures were published in the *Reading Mercury*, Goring's health-improving claims remained localised.

Goring's most noteworthy building is its church with its grey Norman tower close by the river. Apart from its antiquity—more convincing internally than its plastered exterior suggests—it has the distinction of having been built by Robert d'Oilly, who had personally taken part in the Conquest ... which prompts the possibility that, as a contingent of the Conqueror's victorious army passed through Goring on its circuitous route from Hastings to London, d'Oilly may have noted the place as the site of a future church even before his Duke became King.

The tower with its original groining and much of the nave survive from d'Oilly's work, but though his church had the then-customary semi-circular apse at its eastern end the one that now completes the church is a Victorian reconstruction. It has a long and somewhat intricate story. About 1130 a house of Augustinian nuns was established at Goring, the parish church serving also as their church. The arrangement, however, proved unsatisfactory to the nuns; so alongside d'Oilly's church was built one for them separated by an arcade of massive pillars and slightly pointed arches, the arcade that now separates nave from north aisle. Above it the cleres-

tory windows show in their odd placing that they are survivals from
d'Oilly's north wall through which the arcade had to be cut. However the nuns, truly feminine, were still not satisfied, so about 1300
the Norman apse was destroyed in order to build a new church for
the nuns at the east end. The chancel of the parish church, shortened
by the loss of its apse, then ended in a mere stone screen. By that
time the nunnery buildings clustered on three sides of the church;
the corbels on the south wall from which sprang the cloister roof
are the only traces left.

The building of the nuns' church was the high point of the nunnery's history. Though only modestly endowed, it housed thirty-six
nuns. But the fourteenth-century records tell of dissensions among
the nuns, of rival factions disputing the election of the prioress—on
one occasion the two parties meeting in the church for service each
sang the *Te Deum* at the tops of their voices to show their hostility
to the other—and bishops' visitations demanded that their Rule
should be more strictly followed, that the nuns should keep inside
their nunnery and that 'unauthorised strangers' should be refused
admittance. By 1517 the priory was reported as too poor to keep
the buildings in repair. Henry VIII's commissioner, putting into
effect the royal inquiry into the state of religious houses in anticipation of their closure, found only the prioress, three nuns and four
lay sisters in the place. It was then valued at £63 a year, enough to
show the royal exchequer a profit after paying the pensions of £3
to £5 allowed to nuns according to rank and length of service (at a
time when a labourer had to keep his family on about £6 a year).

After the Dissolution the nunnery buildings, including the nuns'
church, were used—as so often happened—as quarries for the locals.
The east end of the parish church, long bereft of its apse, was walled
up ... until 1886 when the foundations of the apse were discovered
under those of the nuns' church and it was decided to rebuild
the east end as it had been in d'Oilly's time. The result can be seen
today.

The church has collected through its long life some items of
note. Hanging as a curiosity above the tower arch is one of the
oldest bells in England. Its Latin inscription tells that it was cast
in London for Peter de Quivil, Bishop of Exeter from 1280 to 1291,
but how it came to Goring is something of a puzzle. The most likely
theory is that the Abbess of Goring from 1283 to 1298 being Sarah
of Exeter and possibly a kinswoman of the bishop, it was given in
the nature of a family present. Certainly the bell was at Goring

early in the fourteenth century; when, in 1929, the other bells were recast and rehung, this oldest bell was left untouched and, as a distinction, placed on show.

There are also five brasses in the church, the earliest being dated 1375. The most interesting is that to Elizabeth Loveday who died in 1401; the inscription is in English, unexpected at so early a date.

At the time Goring church was built the Icknield Way—as yet singular—must have passed very close to it. Now we must look for it at Cleeve, a half-mile along B 4009 from Goring station. There a right turn sign-posted 'Woodcote and Ipsden' and then a left sign-posted only 'Ipsden' and labelled 'Icknield Road', and we are on our way.

This lane prelude to the first official stretch of Icknield is not quite what Goring might have led us to expect. It is suddenly crossing curiously open country. Wide, all but hedgeless cornfields swell and tumble over abrupt hills almost without pattern. They seem neither part of the escarpment rising a mile or so ahead to the east nor of the plain beginning to spread away to the north, and at times they bulge so sharply that fragments of slopes have had to be left unploughed. No doubt it is all the outcome of struggles between chalk and water in geological times when the incipient Thames, hugely swollen by inundations or glacial meltwater, strove to find a way through what has become the Goring gap. It forms a fitting introduction to Icknield for as each bulge is topped the line of the Chilterns is seen reaching away northeast, massing above Ipsden to begin the long escarpment. It is also an unexpectedly quiet country, the narrow lane bouncing up and down across a landscape all but empty of buildings. Here and there a farm, one appropriately called 'Lonesome Farm', breaks the sweeping patchwork of brown and green and, in late summer, sand-coloured corn.

About three miles along the lane stands Icknield Farm, a prim, red-brick building reminiscent more of the enclosures of Victorian times than of any earlier date in Icknield's long history. A little farther at Kaffirs Farm, the Icknield Way achieves recognition on the map; but for those intending to follow it on foot, stout boots and determination will be needed for the first mile. As the lane bears off slightly eastwards, Icknield continues straight on to fringe a field and has been so nearly ploughed up as to make for heavy going; the determination will be called for along the half-mile after the Wallingford–Reading road has been crossed for there the Way has

become smothered in a strip of growth in which blackthorn and brambles predominate. It is an uncomfortable start to what is for so much of its length a green lane; but shortly before the Ipsden lane is reached it brings an unexpected reward. Almost hidden under the blackthorns is a curious monument, a small obelisk on which can be made out the name: JOHN THURLOW READE and the date: NOVEMBER 1827. (The rest of the inscription will baffle anyone unfamiliar with Hindustani.) It has a strange story which will appeal to those who delight in the occult, the mysterious or the merely odd.

The Reade family, about whose most noteworthy member more will be said when Ipsden is reached, have owned the land hereabouts since Tudor times, and the story is told that one of the daughters, in November 1827, was walking along this stretch of Icknield Way when she saw an apparition of one of her brothers who was then living in India. So strong was her conviction that the apparition implied his death that a memorial service was held to him in Ipsden church several days before the news of his death reached the family. The obelisk marks the spot at which the premonition came to the girl. According to his taste for such stories the traveller must make up his mind whether to risk a few scratches to see the sight. Otherwise, a pace across the lane starts the first stretch of green track that is to be characteristic of so much of the Icknield Ways.

From that point can be seen the beginnings of Ipsden, the only village in this curious, many-humped land: a farm, a row of thatch-and-brick cottages and opposite them a timber-and-brick granary still on its mushroom-shaped staddles to baffle thieving rats. Ipsden is, appropriately, an odd little place, its houses shared between two hollows, its church set half a mile away on the far side of a ridge, and all about it little hills that give wide views of the Chilterns tilting towards the Thames or building up into the first tree-capped hills of the escarpment. It is possible to drive through the place without noticing that it is there and certainly unaware that it has three claims to distinction: its name, its church clearly Norman in origin, and its manor-house, the home of the Victorian novelist, Charles Reade.

According to the Place-Name Society Ipsden owes its name to an otherwise undistinguished Saxon called Ippa. According to local tradition the name remembers Bishop Birinus who, if the dates given in the Anglo-Saxon Chronicle can be relied upon, converted the

West Saxons to Christianity within a year of his arrival from Rome in 634. The name Ipsden, they say, is a corruption of 'Bishop's den' (Bishop's hill), and they point to Beren's Hill, a Chiltern crest a mile to the east of the village, as remembering in a slightly corrupted form Birinus' name. They can also point to the fact, recorded in the Anglo-Saxon Chronicle, that for the centre of his newly-acquired bishopric Birinus was granted nearby Dorchester-on-Thames. The visitor must decide between erudition and the less impersonal tradition.

Ipsden church was originally built about 1200 but it suggests little of the impressiveness which 'late Norman' can achieve. It looks as if it was from the beginning only a small village church and has benefited little from the many changes since its flint walls were first built. Its south aisle has been pulled down, the arcade blocked up and rather poor windows inserted, probably late in the fifteenth century. Inside it is plain with little to show; its only brass, dated 1525, is an old one re-used, a palimpsest to the ecclesiologist. But if its out-of-the-way situation attracted no wealthy patrons, it seems that zealous reformers passed it by, too. Besides a Bible of 1660, it possesses a Book of Common Prayer in which are prayers for 'King Charles, Queen Mary, Prince Charles and the rest of the royal Progenie'. The more puritanical of Cromwell's supporters would have been shocked that such a Prayer Book had survived.

A hundred years before Cromwell's time a Thomas Reade of Abingdon, whose family had probably thrived on the wool trade, bought Ipsden, its lands then stretching from the Thames to Stoke Row up in the hills. The house he built has disappeared, but about 1685 one of his descendants built what is now Ipsden House. Of warm brick, and with the additions of 1764 and some remodelling of 1821 all blending, it is still owned by the Reade family. It stands, neat and very English, looking across the fieldscape reaching to the river; its back—which is seen from the lane—forms three sides of its original yard and though some of its former coach-houses serve as garages, its original donkey-wheel has survived from the days when the household water was supplied from a well so deep as to make raising the water a laborious business. From Stuart times, too, survives its round dovecote built for 600 birds and still housing its original revolving ladder by which access could be gained to the nesting boxes built into the walls.

It was in this house that in 1814 Charles Reade was born, the youngest of eleven children. Much of his childhood was spent there

for his early education was undertaken by an older sister. Though in the glimpses of his family life that appear in his *Memoirs* there are few hints of unhappiness, he has little favourable to say of the house itself. To us it looks welcoming; to him it was 'probably the coldest house in Europe ... fires were all but unknown luxuries in its bedrooms; the halls and principal staircases were icy, and even in the living rooms the beechen logs with their cheerful blaze emitted a minimum of heat'. Guests and the family spent their indoors time 'clustered round the hearthrug in the drawing-room'.

Having at last been sent away to school, young Charles Reade seems to have found little desire to return to such a house. He also seems to have found it very difficult to settle into any occupation, trying in succession the law, education and medicine (he refused to please his mother by taking Holy Orders), and at thirty-six he wrote of himself that he 'had done nothing—nothing but learn to play the fiddle and dance the hornpipe ... then, at an age when most men's habits are fixed, I began my real life'. His father's failing health had called him back to Ipsden and there he began on the work that was to lead him to become, in his own time and for a generation or two afterwards, an outstanding novelist.

Few authors have worked so methodically and so painstakingly. Over the years Reade collected a huge amount of detailed information on the subjects on which he wished to write, filling voluminous notebooks with extracts from authoritative works and cuttings from newspapers, and indexing these with such thoroughness that it is said he had to use an index to his indexes. When he set to work on such a book as *It is Never too Late to Mend*, which attacks the harsh contemporary prison conditions, or *Hard Cash*, which deals with the appalling treatment of mental patients, he had hundreds of reports and cuttings and eye-witness accounts to provide him with the background; when he ventured into historical romance with *The Cloister and the Hearth* he had at hand detailed notes on almost every facet of late Medieval life. And yet, when reading a few pages of one of his books, one cannot help wondering if his industry and his desire for authenticity did not let him down. Here and there are memorable scenes, but too often his dramatic moments become merely melodramatic. One comes to suspect that his imagination was not up to his conscientiousness, that he was only truly at ease when retelling an incident which had actually happened or setting a scene for which he could use a pastiche of items from his notebooks. For all his immense industry and the popularity that

his books enjoyed in his lifetime and for a generation afterwards, in the more general picture of Victorian literature he has shrunk to a minor figure—though, like the towering Dickens, he often used his skill and his standing to warn his educated reading public that all was far from well in the society they were creating.

There is another 'memorial' to the Reade family in the Druid Stones a short way above the house, beyond the village football field. The diminutive Stonehenge was built in 1827 as a joke, by one of Charles Reade's brothers.

The Icknield Way, still singular and a grassy track, has made its quiet way a half-mile to the west of Ipsden. A mile north of the village it becomes the lane linking Ipsden to the Wallingford–Henley road; but before then it crosses that tantalising earthwork, Grim's Dyke.

This first view of the Dyke is somewhat misleading. As has been mentioned, there are along the Chilterns other bank-and-ditch earthworks also marked on the map as Grim's Dyke or Grim's Ditch, notably southeast of Risborough and south of Tring; but unlike those puzzlingly angular stretches these first four miles are very straight. With almost Roman precision—though so humble a work has never been attributed to the Romans—here Grim's Dyke carves a line from the Thames about a mile south of Wallingford to Nuffield nearly seven hundred feet up on the crest. It may once have gone much farther, for southeast of Nettlebed its line is taken up by Highmoor Trench (for those who can find it under its thick cover of nettles, thorns and bushes), and a thirteenth-century charter refers to a dyke in Henley parish ... all of which has suggested a defensive work, or at least a boundary protecting the area contained in the southward loop of the Thames.

And there we run up against the first of the many puzzles about Grim's Dyke. It is a crucial assertion of experts on such earthworks that the ditch must be on the side of the bank most likely to be attacked, so that the enemy had first to cross its muddy obstruction before tackling the palisade which is assumed to have surmounted the bank. For this stretch of Grim's Dyke to have served such a purpose, the ditch would have been on the northern side of the bank. It is on the southern side. It would, of course, be possible to overcome such an inconvenience to theory by assuming that the Dyke was intended to defend against attack from the south—until a glance at the map shows that an enemy could have very easily rendered it useless by approaching via the Thames crossing that

gives Wallingford its name, while its eastern end would have failed to cover an attack from the east. All told, as a defensive work it appears to face the wrong way—and that, as we shall see later, is typical of the various fragments of Grim's Dyke elsewhere in the Chilterns.

For the time being the Dyke and its puzzles will have to wait. Barely half a mile ahead the Icknield route crosses the main road from Wallingford to Henley. A fine road it is, climbing boldly up over the ridge to make a long descent through beechwoods to the outskirts of Henley. But before going on, time should be found to venture up one or two of the lanes that lead up into the hills.

Checkendon up on the crest above Ipsden should be a priority. Any of the three lanes climbing southeast from Ipsden will reach it; the best is probably the most southerly which curves its way gradually up a bottom only breaking through the beechwoods as the crest is reached. A right turn in the cluster of houses that comprise most of Checkendon village leads to Checkendon church.

Again it is Norman. That so many churches hereabouts can show much of their Norman work is, however, not due to any medieval love of the past but more to poverty. For all the seemingly rich appearance of the countryside now—and thick woods often give an impression of well-being—this southernmost part of the Chilterns was never a wealthy part of the country. It saw little if anything of the medieval wool trade which brought wealth and fine churches to East Anglia and the Cotswolds; nor did it share, except indirectly, in that other period of suddenly growing prosperity for some, the Industrial Revolution—for which we may be thankful. Ever since its first Saxon colonisers made their way into it, it has remained a quiet, rural and agriculturally rather poor area. Its churches were for the most part built—or rebuilt if we can assume that wooden Saxon churches preceded them—during the decades following the Conquest when the foreign Normans had to impress the native English with their religious zeal as well as their military ability and, with modifications necessitated by natural decay, those churches have had to serve ever since.

Even as one approaches Checkendon church, its Normanness is unmistakable. The rounded apse at the east end and the unplastered walls showing the bands of flints making a herringbone pattern—

perhaps, as a notice in the church porch suggests, the work of Saxon builders during the first generation after the Conquest—look almost untouched since the place was new. Here and there, as we might expect, a later window has allowed more light than the un-glazed Norman windows would have done. Inside the narrow nave has retained that earliness, its fine double Norman chancel arch and the groining to the chancel. In that chancel is a rare medieval addition: a fresco of Christ and the Apostles—though two of them have been lost by the making of a window in the fifteenth century. The painting has had to be restored a little, but it retains its original feeling; its simple, near-outline figures were painted before the heavy, often gruesome 'Dooms' that came in during the century following the Black Death. Checkendon's artist, like its architect (if it had one), had lived in less uneasy times.

Near the church are most of the best of Checkendon's few houses —except perhaps for Basset Manor a mile and a half along the lane to Stoke Row. Timber-framed, with brick nogging and tall chimneys, Basset Manor is essentially Elizabethan, very well preserved.

Whether the traveller continues on to Stoke Row may depend on the season. For most of the year it is unremarkable, a somewhat straggling collection of cottages. Its most noteworthy building is the Maharajah's Well built in 1864 as a gift of the Maharajah of Benares, who learnt from one of the Reade family how short the village was of water, and so provided the dark-green, domed, un-English building that adds only a touch of oddness to the place. But for a week or two in April Stoke Row becomes almost un-believably lovely. The elderly, twisted trees in nearly every garden that in any other month the visitor might hardly notice suddenly show themselves to be cherry-trees and for too short a time their blossoming transforms the village. Passing motorists stop in wonder and clutch their cameras.

Or, from Checkendon, one can go southwards through Woodcote, a scattered, random place of older foundation than it appears, to Whitchurch on the Thames which is neither scattered nor random, its single street of eighteenth- and nineteenth-century houses appear-ing almost compressed between its hill and its bridge. Whichever way the traveller chooses he will make his way through beechwoods and if he has not yet experienced a beechwood he should somewhere stop and do so.

Of course even strangers to the Chilterns will believe that they know a beechwood when they see one. They have probably glimpsed

a few in their travels, or seen a photograph in some magazine devoted to the English countryside, or will if they are old enough
remember those lurid attempts to depict 'Bluebell Time' or 'Autumn
Tints' which used to appear in almost every 'art' shop and are still to
be found in a few. But for the inexperienced it must be said that
a beechwood is more than a visual impression.

The multitude of slim, silver-grey trunks is what catches the
attention at first, and the way they appear to reach almost as far
as the sight will go; and then, according to season, the blue or green
or copper ground and, far overhead, the canopy of pale green or
the tracery of delicate branch and twig. But when one takes a few
steps into the wood, one becomes aware of more than is to be
seen.

The nature of the beech tree, with its spreading, surface-covering
root system and its stretching growth that leaves the trunk almost
without subsidiary branches until far above eye-level, discourages
any but low-growing plants, such as bluebells and wood anemones
and mosses, from thriving within its shade. In a beechwood there
is almost no undergrowth, rarely more than a random holly or a
juniper to break the space that seems to spread around and between
the trunks. And this has limited bird-life to the topmost branches,
where the chiff-chaff will persistently announce its arrival in spring
and tits will through the summer make their sibilant chirping. A
blackbird may, if disturbed, dart squawking between the trunks,
finches and the ubiquitous robin may use briefly the outermost trees,
a woodpecker might nest within a tree-trunk close to the wood's edge.
But these emphasise rather than detract from the stillness that
seems to pervade a beechwood. Even on the windiest day that impression of stillness lingers, a stillness that is to be found in no
other kind of woodland or indeed anywhere else. It is at once restful
and strange. It seems to withstand the sounds from beyond the
wood's edge, the buzz of passing traffic, the wind sweeping across
the adjoining fields, even the rustling in its own tree-tops. The
hackneyed simile likening a beechwood to a cathedral, so often
assumed to refer only to the visual effect, is truer of that feeling
of stillness. A few steps into a beechwood can bring a rare experience for these days, a feeling of awe.

Having reached the river at Whitchurch, there is Mapledurham
only two miles downstream for the walker, though nearer five miles
for the motorist. The walker will pass by Hardwick House, its park

sloping down to the river. Mellow red-brick Tudor (though its cellars are said to date from about 1400), its windows still with their stone mullions, its gables reaching upwards and the whole topped with the clock-tower, it was once the home of Richard Lybbe (whose tomb can be seen in Whitchurch's rather too thoroughly restored church). He was one of the more successful politicians of Tudor times whose religious beliefs were pliable enough for him to win the favour of both Queen Mary and Queen Elizabeth—though perhaps Queen Mary had some doubts for she appointed him taster of the royal dishes, an honour devised to prevent the poisoning of royalty. In Queen Elizabeth's time he had the expensive honour of entertaining Her Majesty at Hardwick House and the room she used still retains her portrait on one of the ceiling bosses from the time when it was redecorated in readiness for her visit.

For the walker the lane leads on beside the river to Mapledurham; the motorist has to climb up to Whitchurch Hill and then cross Goring Heath before he finds the lane that twists down to the village hidden away beside the Thames.

'Mapledreham' the Saxons called it, the homestead by the maple tree, and though its maple has long since gone, it is still all but hidden by trees: willows along the water's edge, elms and cedars about the manor-house, oak and ash and hawthorn in the hedges reaching up to the hill-top beeches. Where a bottom levels as it reaches the river cluster a few cottages, a row of brick-and-flint almshouses, a wooden watermill, an old church with half-hidden behind it the manor-house. In the past many artists, and recently more photographers, have tried to record Mapledurham's many attractions (though one of these, the wooden mill-wheel, is no longer there).

The manor-house, occasionally open to the public during the summer months, was originally an early fifteenth-century, timber-framed house which was partly replaced in the year of the Armada by a brick mansion. Its main front, facing away from the village, has hardly been touched since. In warm brick, it forms the E-shaped plan of the time, with a fine gable to each wing and another over the main entrance. The lofty chimneys, the neat parapets, the stone-mullioned windows—they are all as they were when the house welcomed Queen Elizabeth on one of her many and costly tours; as they were when, during the Civil War, the house was held for the King and, though finally taken by the Parliamentarians, suffered little damage. Even before those days, it was the home of the

Blount family and it still belongs to their descendants. And it has acquired both a priests' hole and a ghost. The hiding-place, fashioned in Elizabethan times when Catholic priests were suspected, sometimes rightly, of association with the enemy Spain, is said to have been connected by a secret passage to the south aisle of the nearby church from which a door, now kept locked, gave access to the river and a precarious freedom. The ghost is that of an eighteenth-century Blount who, in a violent temper, killed a servant and can still, so it is said, be heard dragging the body about the house.

Nowadays the house is remembered also for its associations with the poet, Alexander Pope. It is not easy to imagine him in remote Mapledurham: the oustanding satirist who attacked the society of his day in immaculate verse, and a man 'puny, ill-made, venomous, unjust, splenetic' would seem more a figure of the smart and some-times savage eighteenth-century London society. His association with Mapledurham should remind us that his ill-formed body hid a gentler nature than his satires suggest.

For it was one of the Blount daughters, Martha, fair, gay and light of heart—so she appears in her portraits in Mapledurham House—who drew him again and again to this quiet and restful place. Though his twisted body made it improbable that their friend-ship should ever develop into love, we can gather from his writings that the cripple felt much as any man, though he could express his feelings only with pen and ink. For publication, he wrote his gently chiding complaint on Martha's leaving town:

> As some fond virgin, whom her mother's care
> Drags from the town to wholsom country air,
> Just when she learns to roll a melting eye,
> And hear a spark, yet think no danger nigh ...
> She went from Op'ra, park, assembly, play,
> To morning walks and prayers three times a day,
> To part her time 'twixt reading and bohea,
> To muse, and spill her solitary tea,
> Or o'er cold coffee trifle with the spoon,
> Count the slow clock, and dine exact at noon;
> Divert her eyes with pictures in the fire,
> Hum half a tune, tell stories to the squire....

More privately, he wrote in a book he gave her:

> Each pretty carecter with pleasing smart,
> Deepens the dear Idea in my heart.

And, on a day in October 1711, scribbled a brief note:

> My poor Father dyed last night. Believe, since I don't forget you this
> moment, I never shall.
>
> A. POPE

His love for Martha Blount was no transient whim of youth and subject of a few gay or plaintive lyrics. It lasted in letters, poems, and meetings through his whole life, and when he died he left her, besides a thousand pounds, his plate and his books.

Internally Mapledurham church is more curious than attractive. Originally built about 1200, it was much altered late in the fourteenth century and was restored in 1862 when an aisle separated by two wooden pillars was formed, and twenty-five feet and a somewhat heavy cap were added to its tower. It has fragments of old glass, a good brass of 1395 to Sir Robert Bardolph, a former owner of the manor-house and, curtained off from the rest of the church, a south aisle that served as the Blount family chapel—in its day an unexpectedly tolerant arrangement, for the Blounts were Roman Catholics.

Another poet is remembered downstream—though the car traveller would be wise to skirt north of Caversham to get there. At Shiplake, halfway between Reading and Henley, Tennyson was married after a courtship lasting over twelve years. He had first met Emily Sellwood in his native Lincolnshire when she was seventeen and he was twenty-one. They met again six years later, when she was a bridesmaid at his brother's wedding to her sister, and Tennyson fell deeply in love with her. But he was still an unknown and penurious poet and Emily would never have allowed him to give up his poetry for a more secure source of income. After two years their engagement was broken off and they remained out of touch for ten years, ten years in which he was to develop as a poet until he produced his greatest work, *In Memoriam*, the royalty from which, plus a bank loan of £300, made marriage possible. A friend brought them together at Shiplake and there in June 1850 they were married. A few months later Tennyson was offered the Poet Laureateship; thereafter wealth was his and fame during his lifetime. Later generations while still admiring his technique—few poets have achieved his mastery of the rhythms and the sounds of words which make his poems 'verbal melodies'—may find his later poetry hints too often of Victorian values and shortcomings. Perhaps it is not

inappropriate that Shiplake church has since Tennyson's wedding day been thoroughly restored according to Victorian ideas. The present south aisle which was the original nave and the tower which was in Tennyson's day detached from the church have survived; the glass, medieval, from the Abbey of St. Bertin near Calais (and hidden by the monks during the French Revolution), was given to Shiplake in 1830, and a sixteenth-century brass still survives. But much of the feeling of the church that Tennyson knew, and Miss Mitford described in *Our Village*, has gone.

Henley is only two miles from Shiplake; whether it regards itself as a Chiltern town or not, the approach from Shiplake does not do it justice. So back to Icknield for an alternative way through the hills.

Just before reaching the Wallingford–Henley road, a lane leads from the Icknield Way up to Nuffield. Unlike most lanes that climb up to the crest it follows not a bottom but a spur, rising quickly and then giving views on either side of the combes in the escarpment. Nuffield, which via William Morris of car fame has given its name to an Oxford college, is a little hill-top place with a church, small and once Norman, which retains its original font, embellished with the rarity of a Latin inscription, for which a note in the church offers the translation: 'Go wash in a sacred place; either grace cleanses the whole, or cleansing by the font is not complete.'

Across Nuffield Common, now mostly a golf course, the main road leads through Nettlebed—whose name, first recorded in 1246, rather unexpectedly is not a corruption of something else but means what it says. From there a road leads southwards through beech-woods to Rotherfield Greys and Rotherfield Peppard.

The 'Rotherfield', the Saxon's 'open land where cattle graze', must once have been extensive; it was, in the thirteenth century, shared between the Grey and the Pipard families. Some of that 'open land' remains in Rotherfield Peppard's wide common with its tree-clusters and unexpected, suddenly deep hollows.

Rotherfield Greys lies between Peppard and Henley, a somewhat scattered village, its centre seeming to be the green on which in summer cricket is played as it originated, a game of competing villages rather than an occupation of professionals in town surroundings.

Rotherfield Greys' sight is Greys Court, a fragment of the fourteenth-century castle of the Greys in the original courtyard of which

was built first the great house of the Knollys family of Elizabethan times and, when that had been destroyed in the Civil War, a late-Stuart house which is not a noteworthy example of its period. The result, more interesting for its associations than for its architecture, is open to the public on three days a week during the summer.

Of the castle for which John de Grey obtained 'licence to crenellate' in 1348, the great square tower, three of the four octagonal corner towers and a portion of the curtain wall remain, built of flint and brick—an early example of the revival of brick-building with thin bricks suggesting an imitation of the Roman.

The Greys were succeeded by the Lovells of whose family is told the tale of 'Mistletoe Bough'—the melancholy story in verse was a Victorian favourite—and the wooden chest in which the bride is said to have hidden and, undiscovered, to have died used to be shown at Greys Court. When, after the failure at Stoke to unseat the new Henry VII, the last Lord Lovell disappeared—according to the story at Minster Lovell by hiding in a locked cellar there and being starved to death when the only servant in the know inopportunely died—the Greys' castle passed to the rising family of the Knollys, who later built the Elizabethan house. All that remains of this is the range of stables, little altered since, and the well-house with its donkey-wheel.

The Knollys' occupancy was somewhat chequered. The first Knollys was Francis, treasurer and cousin-in-law to Queen Elizabeth, whose loyalty and determined Protestantism made him the ideal custodian of Mary, Queen of Scots, when she fled from the wrath of Knox's supporters to seek refuge in her royal cousin's England. So seriously did Knollys take his duties that he persuaded Mary to read the English Prayer Book—without noticeable effect.

Knollys' son and successor, William, served both Elizabeth and James I and was rewarded with the earldom of Banbury. But at the age of fifty-eight, his second marriage to the nineteen-year-old Elizabeth Howard disturbed the peace he had known at Rother-field Greys. She soon tired of her elderly husband and was so indiscreet in her scandals that her sons were forbidden to succeed to the earldom. Meanwhile her sister, Frances Howard, young wife of the Earl of Essex, showed similar tendencies by becoming involved with King James's favourite, Robert Carr, Earl of Somerset. The King ordered William Knollys to detain Frances and her husband at Greys Court—as if William had not, in his own wife, enough to cope with. The double task apparently proved too much for him,

for Frances succeeded in divorcing her husband and marrying her lover against opposition in which her sternest critic was Sir Thomas Overbury. When he died suddenly and conveniently Frances and Carr were charged with murder by poisoning. After four years in the Tower of London, they were returned to Greys Court under restraint, but their arrival did not lessen William's worries. Love had turned to violent hatred, and Frances and Carr insisted that they should be lodged in separate towers—to which William must have agreed with relief.

The Knollys, Francis and William, are remembered in Rotherfield Greys church: north of the chancel is the family chapel built by William in 1605. Dominating the other monuments stands the elaborate and colourful tomb erected by William for his father and mother (who was, as Queen Elizabeth's cousin and friend, in fact buried at Westminster). Their effigies lie dressed in full Elizabethan splendour; on one side kneel their seven sons and on the other their six daughters—and in red, in contrast with the girls' blue dresses, Dorothy, first wife of William. Above the recumbent figures William himself appears, diminutive and piously kneeling, together with his second wife, the wayward Elizabeth.

This chapel was added to the Greys' church, which had been a remodelling of an earlier Norman one. The last of that family, Sir Robert de Grey, who died in 1387, lies in the tomb in the chancel. The fine brass, perhaps ordered by him during his lifetime, shows him in full armour of the style of his young manhood.

From Greys Court a lane leads down to Henley, entering the town at the top of its market-place with the wide main street leading on to its church and bridge. The church, well known to all who have enjoyed Henley's reach and the famous regatta course, has been enlarged more than once since it was first built in the fourteenth century, and tends to be for all its size and dignity rather unwelcoming. It has, however, some noteworthy monuments, one to a sister of Francis Bacon, and another to General Dumouriez who, having served in the Seven Years' War and gained Louis XV's favour, contrived to become Foreign Minister and a popular hero under the Revolution, only to find it necessary under Napoleon to flee to England where he contributed to the British war effort that ended at Waterloo—and finally came to rest in very English Henley.

Behind the church is the fifteenth-century Chantry House (and one-time school); few visitors find it. Opposite the church is a group of timber-framed houses—and the observant may notice that some

of their timbers have been re-used; it was a former custom, when ships were being dismantled in London River, for the timbers to be towed upstream to serve as house-frames. One of this group (now a tea-shop) was the home of William Lenthall, Speaker of the House of Commons on what must have been the House's most dramatic occasion: Charles I's armed intrusion to demand the hiding-places of the rebellious and famous Five Members who were guiding the country towards civil war: 'I have neither eyes to see nor tongue to speak in this place, but as the House is pleased to direct me,' was Lenthall's often-quoted evasion—and the breach between King and Parliament had become dangerously wide.

Other houses of seventeenth- and eighteenth-century date are to be found in Henley's pleasant streets. In one house lurk strange memories. There lived Mary Blandy, the 'murdered maid' who in the 1750s achieved a brief posthumous fame as an example of the miscarriage of justice. Daughter of a wealthy townsman, she was wooed by a Captain Cranstoun, already married. When her father opposed the association, Cranstoun persuaded the girl to serve Father a charmed drink—which, in keeping with the circumstances, contained a lethal dose of arsenic. Mary was accused, tried, and executed; but popular feeling assumed her innocent at least of the intention to murder, and at elections during the next decade her case was used to 'prove' judicial and therefore governmental short-comings. Though her story has been all but forgotten, old people about Henley may still recall that her ghost, riding a white horse, was said to appear in a lane between Henley and Hambleden.

Such a story hardly fits the Henley of today. Always seeming to be alive and even on the dullest day a bright, friendly place, it would be more fitting to end a visit with a stroll on to its bridge. Behind the town the Chilterns rise, across the river are more beech-topped hills, while downstream stretches the straight mile of the regatta course curving at last beyond the Island Temple under the hills above Hambleden—where soon we shall be calling.

FOUR

'The Deserts of Chiltern'

Ironically it was probably the region of the Chilterns between the Wallingford and the Oxford roads that the seventh-century Saxon monk had in mind when he used the phrase 'the deserts of Chiltern'. For us it is an area of beechwoods, bluebells, and prosperous-looking farms. We must assume that the priest was a companionable man for whom the word 'desert' implied not so much a desolate waste as an area as yet uncultivated and therefore unpeopled. Though at the time he was writing Saxon settlers had reached the Thames between Goring and Henley and had taken over the Icknield strip, the seventy or so square miles in between had seen little prolonged human settlement. Many of the villages there are ancient by our reckoning—Turville is mentioned in the Domesday Book, Fingest has an early Norman church, the hamlet of Skirmett recalls the Danes—but it is likely that they were founded during the four centuries of Saxon England after that priest had written. The earlier Saxon settlers would, no doubt, have seized the open, already cleared land. Only later would the hidden valleys have been penetrated. Even now, the villages are widely spaced and the parishes large.

From the point where the Icknield Way (as yet still singular) crosses the Henley–Wallingford road, it continues slightly east of north as a by-road until after a mile it meets four other lanes on Beggarsbush Hill, a swelling of the land giving a sight of the ridge reaching northwards. There, slightly right, the Way, as a by-road signposted 'Ewelme Down, Swyncombe, Cookley Green', makes towards the escarpment, becomes indisputably the Upper Icknield and within two miles a green lane. Straight on from Beggarsbush Hill and signposted 'Ewelme and Watlington' another by-road edges more northerly—perhaps the beginning of the Lower Icknield Way, for a few miles ahead it dwindles into a sequence of track and footpath and, later, achieves its name on the map.

Whichever lane the traveller chooses he should not overlook Ewelme. Its main group of buildings, obviously medieval in appearance and feeling, is unique.

In those somewhat improbable books that were published from the 1930s until about ten years ago when it was still possible to suggest 'exploring' the 'beauty of Britain'—which meant generally taking somewhat sentimental glances at 'pretty villages'—Ewelme was sure of a mention. Yet its attractions were seldom illustrated; and they rarely achieved the distinction of appearing in those calendars which, rather cloyingly, depicted (and still do) 'Beautiful Britain' or 'Gems of Olde Englande'. Though countless snaps must have been taken there, none attained the repeated publication which makes for immediate recognition. The village is, in fact, very limited photogenically; it does not arrange itself conveniently around a green or Narcissus-like admire itself in its duck-pond; it does not even spread itself along a street to catch the eye of casual passers-by. The tilt of the ground and deliberate seclusion allow the photographer or the passing traveller only a fragmented impression, never a complete shot. To see Ewelme, you have to go there, stop, and look.

On the map the village stands across the arms of three roads which form a rough Y to pass a sharp slope. The tail of the Y leads across Cow Common, the former common land of the place, to the Upper Icknield Way. Across the top of the Y a road (B 4009) links it with Watlington, and with the Thames valley at Benson. Along these roads have been planted brick and flint houses, many of them interesting. But the heart of Ewelme is in the group of fifteenth-century buildings that climbs the rise between the two arms of the Y. And, what makes Ewelme so unusual, the whole group appears to have been scarcely touched since it was completed in about 1470. There must have been occasional necessary attention to the fabric—plaster, brick or stone repaired here and there—but mercifully no Victorian restorer got his hands on the place.

The buildings comprise the church, a quadrangle of almshouses, and a 'free school'. The idea of building them as a whole appears to have originated in the mind of William de la Pole, Duke of Suffolk—and that provides one of those historical surprises that make medieval man so interesting a being. This William de la Pole was the Duke of Suffolk who, as adviser to the young and pathetically unpolitical Henry VI, used his position to add to his already huge wealth while what we know as the Hundred Years'

War dragged on to its final battle. Suffolk was of course not solely responsible either for the sequence of defeats or for the unpopular programme which attempted to salvage something from past victories by arranging a marriage between young Henry VI and Margaret of Anjou (who in her widowhood was later to live at Ewelme); but when a scapegoat was needed he who had been so prominent an adviser to the king was the inevitable choice. The Commons accused him of selling the realm to France and he was sent to the Tower; but when he was allowed to escape the populace in the persons of a party of Dover seamen recognised him and carried out the contemporary idea of justice—with six blows from a rusty sword if tradition is reliable. Hardly the man, it would seem, to find time to think of the poor and elderly or the poor and young; and yet that is what he must have done at Ewelme, though the actual buildings that express his intentions were left to his widow to finish—and they were built at the time when their son John was, as the Paston letters tell us, hiring gangs of toughs to drive peaceable people off their land to which he appears to have had no legal claim.

Such a family set against their memorial at Ewelme seems to us a strange mixture of greed and generosity, of nastiness and thought for others; for if our twentieth-century minds are tempted to regard their gift to Ewelme as a mere expression of a guilty conscience, would not they like others of their time and class have assumed that it was charity enough either to rebuild the church or to provide almshouses for the old or to found a school for Ewelme's poor boys? To have done all three was remarkable even in those days when what we might call superstition could exaggerate any feelings of guilt. The evil that Suffolk did may live after him in the history books but the good he intended was not wholly 'interred with his bones', as Ewelme has shown for five hundred years.

Approaching from the south, the first building is the school, impressively tall, of stone and mellow brick, with two lofty external chimney-stacks. It is still used as a school (primary) and, if the visitor chooses his time suitably, he may be allowed to see that the upper school room still has its original roof and an array of carved heads and shields over its windows below which the village children are still taught, as the Duke and Duchess intended, 'freely without exaccion of any schole hire'.

Above the school and adjoining its upper side—and easily missed by hasty passers-by—is the quadrangle of brick and timber alms-

houses. The main entrance is on the uphill path, a fine double gateway in brick embellished with a pattern imitating stone tracery. The entry more usually open to visitors is the doorway in the adjoining church tower (the only surviving part of an earlier church). From there a flight of steps leads down to the square court around the covered walk of which stand the secluded homes provided for thirteen old men and women for the past five hundred years—and should a visit coincide with that of some middle-aged and sentimental sightseer you may overhear that she 'wouldn't mind' ending her days 'in such a peaceful place'.

The church itself appears, architecturally, a little meagre. Built during the last decades before the change in religious outlook that was to bring about the Reformation—that is, 'late Perp.' according to the guidebooks—it makes one wonder how church architecture would have developed had not wayward Henry VIII quarrelled with the Pope of his day. By the time Ewelme church was being built the urge that had revived the Gothic style after the Black Death and produced the peculiarly English Perpendicular variation with its triumphs in a score of East Anglian and West Country 'wool churches' was beginning to wane. Noticeable most in Ewelme's arcades and windows which nearly approach the rectangular there is a lack of inspiration. Yet the church has much to show—and first, perhaps, there should be a grateful glance towards the wall-monument that recalls Colonel Francis Martyn who commanded the Parliamentary forces stationed at Ewelme during the Civil War and restrained the more zealous Puritans among his men from defacing the church.

It is rare to find a medieval church with so much of its original fittings intact and therefore able to give a more real impression of what it had been and what it had meant in the days of its building. The roof and most of the woodwork including the font cover, an amazing piece of craftsmanship, have survived. In St John's chapel at the east end of the south aisle and intended for the residents of the almshouses, the carved screens, much of the glass and even the floor tiles are as old as the building. They make a setting fit for the church's two show-pieces, the tombs of Suffolk's Duchess and her parents, Thomas and Maud Chaucer.

Both tombs are perfect examples of their period. Under a canopy of intricate stonework—a visitor could spend a half-hour studying its details—the Duchess Alice is depicted wearing her coronet and the Garter while below through a stone grille lies her cadaver, for

9. Ickleford, on the 'Icknield strip'

CHILTERN VILLAGES

10. Westmill, near the Cambridge Road

*11. Flint, circa 1100, at
Checkendon*

*12. Timber, plaster a
thatch, circa 1700,
Aspenden*

the medieval mind faced the reality of death with less evasiveness than we tend to do. Today's visitors often linger longer at her parents' tomb, simpler, of dark marble, with the figures as brasses, he in plate armour, his widow in wimple, veil and close-fitting kirtle. The sides of the tomb are brightened with a design of enamelled shields, a display that anyone with only the slightest feeling for heraldry must admire and which must delight the expert.

This Thomas Chaucer is believed to have been the poet's son, though contemporary records tell nothing of Geoffrey Chaucer's family-life but that his wife's name was Philippa. The poet himself refers only to his 'litel sone' Lewis for whom he wrote his 'Treatise on the Astrolabe'. Not until about thirty years after the poet's death does a solitary statement link Geoffrey and Thomas; the Chancellor of Oxford, Thomas Gascoigne, who died in 1458, mentions that the poet was father of Thomas Chaucer, knight, of Ewelme near Oxford. So belated a reference seems a little odd at a time when parentage counted for so much, and we know quite a lot about Thomas Chaucer, who married Maud Burghersh, heiress of Ewelme. He was a man of wealth and importance who fought at Agincourt, sat in no less than fourteen Parliaments, acting the Speaker in some of them, and was honoured with the appointment of royal Chief Butler. We know, too, that his mother was Philippa de Roet, sister to Katherine, wife of Thomas Swinford, who became John of Gaunt's third wife. We know that Thomas Chaucer's only child Alice became, on her third marriage in 1432, the Duchess of Suffolk who lies nearby. Much of this is set out armorially on the Chaucer tomb (and for the convenience of visitors in a named diagram above it); indeed the arms of so many distant relations are featured—Beauforts, Nevilles, Percys and other noble families—that the work hints of medieval name-dropping. But the one coat of arms we really want to see is not there—that of Geoffrey Chaucer himself (which is on his tomb in Westminster Abbey). Could it be that Alice Chaucer having become a duchess did not, when ordering her parents' tomb, wish to own as paternal grandfather a mere poet? This tomb is at times quoted as evidence that the poet's wife was Philippa de Roet; the reasoning is a little insecure but if the visitor's interest in the fine workmanship is heightened by a belief that the tomb holds the remains of Geoffrey Chaucer's only son, only a purist would quibble.

These two remarkable monuments tend to make the visitor over-

look others of interest: no less than seventeen brasses dated from 1454 to 1695, one with an inscription promising, a little presumptuously to our twentieth-century thinking, a hundred days' pardon to those who pray for the occupant of the tomb. Outside in a corner between the church and the almshouses is a stone which forty or so years ago attracted more notice than it does today. It marks the grave of Jerome K. Jerome, author of *The Idle Thoughts of an Idle Fellow* and *Three Men in a Boat* which, selling in hundreds of thousands, drew gusts of innocent laughter from our parents and grandparents. Is it still possible to enjoy his unsophisticated humour, his ability to catch the funniness of everyday weaknesses? Certainly the sentimentality of his more serious efforts shows how our outlook has changed in fifty years.

A hundred and more years before Jerome's time, the name of Ewelme had achieved another distinction: 'Ewelme Watercress!' was cried in the London streets. It was—and still is—grown along the valley leading down to Benson. The streams from the springs issuing from under the chalk have for a long time been known as specially suitable for watercress—as the watchful traveller will notice in several Chiltern valleys.

From Ewelme the B 4009 leads over Firebrass Hill. It is a jaunty road seldom straight or flat for long and at many a rise giving views of the bold line of hills away to the east. For those on foot a path leads from just above Ewelme across the fields to find the Upper Icknield at a corner of the wood below Swyncombe Downs. From there for the six miles to the Oxford road, it is a wide grass track, and so little used as to feel remote. On a summer's day you could walk two or three miles of it with only the rooks and larks in the nearby fields and buntings and finches in the hedges for company.

Ever and again a path or lane links the Way to a village below, the villages through which the motorist following the parallel road will pass. Most are worth more than a glance and many are worth a half-mile's walk across the fields.

The first from Ewelme is Britwell Salome, small, slight, and not so distinctive as its name suggests. Only for visitors does the 'Salome' recall the Bible story or Oscar Wilde's play; for the locals it is pronounced 'So-lem' because in the thirteenth century Almaric de Suleham (Sulham, Berkshire) held the manor. The 'Britwell' is really more interesting; it means not 'bright well' as is often said but 'Britons' well', a reminder that Celtic-speaking people lingered

here after the arrival of the Saxons. If a call should be made at the Red Lion and there are a few minutes to spare, some of the houses in the loop road behind the pub, mellow and old and well cared-for, are worth looking at.

Watlington, the town of the neighbourhood and appropriately small, is a mile and a half farther on. 'Watlington,' says a guide book which has somehow remained in my family's possession since it was written in 1905 for the cyclists who then were the countryside's main tourists, 'Watlington has little to interest the visitor.' That guide book needs to be thrown away—though to be fair to its author in those days the main attraction was always the church and Watlington's suffered a zealous restoration in 1877. One of the few interesting items left in it to hint briefly of its medieval origin is a brass, the figures of which are with fifteenth-century realism depicted in their shrouds. As for the building, the Victorian architect might at least have contrived to make it a little less dark—though then the attempts to give a Norman appearance to the carvings about the capitals of the nave arcade (which once were Norman in truth) would have been even more unconvincing. But as for the rest of Watlington—there is plenty to catch the eye in the narrow, curving streets of eighteenth- and early nineteenth-century shops and houses. They give an impression of warmth with their red brick and red tiles—though here and there show walls of flint and clunch, and even a few thatched roofs. And appropriately at the centre stands the fine, wide-arched market hall dated 1664. All told, a pleasant little town in which, if few buildings are outstanding, even fewer jar on the eye.

Watlington was once quite an important place. It had a castle, though even the moat is now scarcely traceable. As its market hall shows, its streets were once busy with traders. But now it is usually quiet—indeed it often gives the impression that little of more than local significance has happened in the place since that June evening of 1643 when John Hampden lodged here before riding the few miles to Chalgrove Field and his death wound. Several visits to Watlington have left the suspicion that the Watlingtonians enjoy either a very protracted lunch-break or an early closing day six times a week; and that is another of Watlington's attractions. To be within a mere three dozen miles of London as the jet flies and within easy reach of a trunk road and a motorway, and yet to preserve a feeling of apartness from the scrambling 1970s is an achievement.

The lane beside Watlington church leads through the fields to Pyrton, whose church has been treated similarly to Watlington's, though not so drastically. The rich mouldings to the Norman door and chancel are as good as any small church hereabouts can show; but how closely the building as a whole resembles the one in which John Hampden married Elizabeth Symeon on Midsummer Day, 1619, must be left to the visitor's imagination. More certainly real is Elizabeth Symeon's home, Pyrton Manor, standing in seclusion beside its large pond in a park beyond the churchyard. Built some forty years before the Hampdens' wedding day, it still looks, except for 350 years' mellowing of its brickwork, much as they knew it: warm, red, Elizabethan, and wholly delightful.

Opposite Pyrton church are other houses worth more than a glance: the Old Vicarage, eighteenth-century square, tall and of purple and red brick, and a white-plastered house the back of which is older than the bow-windowed front. On along the lane is the village's thatched inn. Here a track leads northeastwards, perhaps an unrecognised stretch of the Lower Icknield for, though the 'Viatores' suggest the road (B 4009), the track is continued as a footpath which heads straight for the Romanised Icknield where it bypasses Aston Rowant across the Oxford Road. The lane-and-footpath is a quiet, easy way skirting Shirburn Park, and in winter the walker might glimpse through the bare trees Shirburn Castle—which is more than the passer-by will see along the Watlington road, from which the building is screened by a high wall, a collection of cottages and outbuildings, and dark evergreens.

Of Norman origin and rebuilt in 1377, Shirburn Castle is the most complete example of medieval military architecture in the whole region, and successive owners have done their best to hide it from view. The few peeps allowed are, however, not encouraging. The square building, still surrounded by its moat, is so smothered with rough cast and has in its 600 years sprouted so many unlikely chimneys and windows, that its appearance is somewhat spurious. Nor is the church which stands off the Watlington road near the castle entrance very rewarding to visitors. Originally Norman, it has suffered so much restoration that architecturally there is little of note; perhaps the most interesting item is a fragment of seventeenth-century wood-carving, probably taken from a tomb and now on a wall in the south transept. It shows Abraham about to sacrifice Isaac with the ram appropriately caught in a thicket nearby; and to the left two men and horses wait, as Stuart servants would have

waited, until their master had finished his business. Hardly a work of art but an interesting period piece.

In the church lies a former owner of the castle: Lord Chancellor Macclesfield, who in George I's time when corruption was almost part of government, so profited from his position that he was accused of corruption, impeached, and found guilty. Thereafter he disappeared from public life and reappeared only once, it is said, when he acted as pall-bearer at the funeral of his former friend, Sir Isaac Newton. In the church lies his son also, a leading astronomer of his day who helped to frame the Bill which, in 1752, brought the calendar up to date: 'Give us back our eleven days!'

Lewknor, a mile-and-a-half farther on, is larger, more interesting, and lies near the hills—though thrusting Beacon Hill is now separated from it by the Oxford motorway where it swings southwards to avoid Aston Hill. The houses and cottages of Lewknor mostly stand in brief by-lanes off the main road, and many of them show the traditional local brick-and-flint.

Lewknor church stands across a playing field a corner of which is the village school playground. The school building fits the village. It appears to have been originally a Victorian house, square, brick-and-flint and symmetrical, to which a lower wing was added on either side to provide the classrooms. Appropriately these wings were built of local brick and flint, and thatched; and they have remained thatched—which suggests that not all local authorities are as rigid in their outlook as is often assumed. During the past century it must have occurred to someone in the county surveyor's department to save the cost of rethatching by giving the school a new and less village-matching roof; but the temptation has been resisted.

The church itself owes much of its interest to the fact that, in medieval times, it was owned by the abbey at Abingdon (for which we may be grateful but the medieval incumbent, denied part of his income by the monastery, might not have been too pleased about it). Like the churches of Watlington and Shirburn, it was first built in the Norman style; but it had the good fortune to be restored in about 1300 and not 1870. The nave arcade, the chancel arch and the massive font with its curious pattern of linked roundels all remain from the church built before 1180. The chancel and the south aisle date from the restoration of 1280 to 1320, a time when the first Early English Gothic style had lost its original austerity and was blossoming into what is called Decorated, a name very appropriate to the stonework in Lewknor's chancel. For historically

55

inclined visitors it is interesting to stand by the pulpit and look first at the austere columns and arches of the Norman nave (fourteenth-century windows behind), and then at the carved stonework, piscina and sedilia, in the chancel. The differences show how the country changed in the century-and-a-half after Henry II's time. Life, at least for some, had become rich enough to afford the skill of such stonemasons but in the process something had been lost of the religious zeal revived by the Cistercian monks and Franciscan friars with the stress on simplicity of building and their initial demand for a turning away from worldly riches. A similar, but later, comparison can be made between the tombs which stand just within the chancel and those visible behind the screen to the north transept, used as the Jodrell family chapel. Though in Stuart dress the figures in the chancel lie in the conventional medieval pose, straight and restful with hands lifted in prayer. The monument that catches the eye in the Jodrell mausoleum tells a story not far removed from those which Victorian children were expected to emulate.

A mile beyond Lewknor is the Oxford road and the limit of this section of the Way.

Before continuing northwards, a few of the lanes that climb over the ridge should be sampled. They lead to those places that grew up within the 'deserts of Chiltern' which Pevsner has called, in the *Buckinghamshire* book of his 'Buildings of England', the 'most secluded and perhaps the most beautiful part of the Chilterns'.

From the road linking the villages already mentioned, the villages of the Icknield strip, many lanes and tracks start off towards the escarpment, but some after crossing the Upper Icknield Way lead only to farms in the shelter of steep-sided combes or dwindle into climbing footpaths. Of the four that persist as metalled roads, narrow, twisting, and before they reach the top steep, three meet above Swyncombe. Standing high up near the head of a combe, little more than a manor-house (rebuilt in Victorian times) and a church originally Norman, Swyncombe can be easily overlooked. Its tilting woods are among the finest in the Chilterns and if its diminutive church has been almost reconstructed, it has contrived to retain its Normanness: dim, small, plain, and consisting, as in its beginning, of only nave and apse-ended chancel.

The homes Swyncombe church serves are grouped round Cookley Green, nearly a mile to the east on the ridge. The Chiltern ridge-

route here crosses the green as an avenue of lime-trees along the B 481 joining Nettlebed and Watlington. Those who follow that route northwards through the beechwoods will now and again catch sight of the farms steeply below and, beyond them, the villages of the Icknield strip. They may learn that the bolder, more thrusting hills of the escarpment are named after the villages—a reminder that while the land about each village grew its grain crops, up here on the crest was the grazing land. The medieval villagers must have thought little of a steep two-mile walk to find 'pannage' for their pigs.

From a little north of Cookley Green two lanes and a selection of paths lead southeasterly towards Stonor deep in a bottom of the hills. For the motorist either lane will do, though they are rather different. One (B 480) dips quickly into a bottom filled with trees and then weaves a way through the hills around Pishill, notable for The Crown, mainly country-Tudor, with its thatched, timbered barn, to reach Stonor from the north. The other lane keeps along a ridge through the hamlets of Russell's Water and Maidensgrove before a sudden descent through the woods into the Stonor bottom.

Mention of Russell's Water raises a major question that keeps cropping up in chalk country: chalk being so porous, how before the days of mains-water did the locals get their water supply? A well was from Saxon times onwards one answer, though a far from easy one: the well served by Greys Court's donkey-wheel is over 200 feet deep, while the Maharajah's gift to Stoke Row is 380 feet deep. Few hilltop hamlets in the early days could have undertaken digging such wells.

Russell's Water offers another answer: its houses, some of them perhaps 200 years old, are grouped round the sizeable pond that gives the place its name. But that merely pushes the question another step further away: How did the pond get there?

Fifty or so years ago it would have been quite safe to talk about 'dew ponds' and the mysteries of their making. Back in the Bronze Age—or was it the New Stone Age?—when the natives grazed their herds and flocks on the bare open downlands, they learnt the secret of making ponds which by some still unexplained means contrived both to last for thousands of years and also, throughout that long stretch, to remain filled by dew.... At least, that was the story and along the Sussex and Berkshire Downs (but rarely the Chilterns) neat, circular ponds which, it was claimed, had never been known to run dry, were pointed out, photographed and generally regarded

with something approaching awe. Such 'mysteries' have now been cleared up. We not only know how 'dew ponds'—in reality supplied by mundane rain—were lined with non-porous clay sometimes bonded with straw, but also, so elderly country-dwellers have asserted, their grandfather's grandfather knew a man who made them back in the 1700s.

And yet, the experts having apparently disposed of both the mystery and the antiquity of 'dew ponds', the puzzle as to how the locals got their water supply has been added to rather than diminished. There are in most chalk uplands indisputable sites of human habitation going back at least 2,500 years, many for twice that time. Though geologists assert that in such a remote time the local water-table was higher than it is now and that bottoms now dry then flowed with streams, that is of little relevance: Russell's Water at well over 500 feet would still have been far above such a water supply. There remains, however, the possibility that its pond —and possibly many another on the Chiltern crest and on chalk hills generally—might have been in part natural. As has been mentioned, many of the higher points of the hills are capped with 'clay-with-flints'. Many such caps are too thin to have retained water, but a thicker layer—and some are known to reach fifty feet—might retain in the form of a shallow, clayey pond much of the rain that fell upon it. As such it would be of little use to, say, a Neolithic cowherd; but hollow out the clay to a depth of a few feet and there would be the beginnings of a 'dew pond'. Of course its clay lining would have to be repaired from time to time, but such a pond in an otherwise unwatered area would have attracted settlement. In his absorbing book, *The Making of the English Landscape*, Professor W. G. Hoskins suspects that this was the origin of villages such as Ashmore, high up on the Dorset chalk-hills, which he says 'has probably been continuously lived in since Romano-British times'.

Russell's Water as it is now does not suggest such antiquity. Its older houses, perhaps of late-eighteenth-century date, offer the probability that it was one of those hamlets which came into being when the common lands were being enclosed (and both it and nearby Maidensgrove have the remains of commons). It was a time of expanding agriculture urged on by new farming techniques when land which had earlier been used merely as rough grazing could be brought under cultivation. And the movement was to continue through the wars with Revolutionary and Napoleonic France which,

by interrupting overseas trade, enhanced farming profits and prompted the Corn Laws. During such times new hamlets—a farm or two, a few labourers' cottages, perhaps an inn and perhaps a nonconformist chapel—came into being and earlier half-forgotten ones were revived and reconstructed. Only detailed study of such records as survive can establish with certainty which farming boom brought such a hamlet as Russell's Water into being. The style of its mellow cottages, now adapted and enlarged into country homes, suggests that we may owe them to Napoleon's attempt to starve Britain, though its neighbour along the same ridge, Maidensgrove, at a glance of similar age and origin, may have been earlier. In the ancient parish of Bix a mile to the south there was in 1431 an area called 'Menygrove', the 'common clearing' of the villagers.

Maidensgrove Common, just before the ridge topples down through beech woods to the Stonor hollow, looks over the richly wooded hills through which curves a bottom to farmlands three miles away below modern Bix on the Henley–Wallingford road. It is a little frequented part which we must take a closer look at.

Below Maidensgrove along the lane lies Stonor, on the B 480 linking Watlington to Henley. It is hardly a village, rather a hamlet stretching a quarter-mile along the road, a few dozen cottages, some old, some recent, and an inn. The parish church is a mile and a half away at Pishill (originally, and less disturbing to the easily embarrassed, 'peas-hill') and almost hidden in the woods. The main sight for the traveller hereabouts is Stonor House, but it is rarely open to the public. Of rich Tudor brick and possessing hiding places fashioned in Elizabeth's time, it can be seen distantly from a footpath starting a hundred yards south of the lodge gates. A motorist will be lucky to catch a glimpse of the place, it is so screened by richly wooded hills which Pope called 'the gloomy verdure of Stonor'—but he was writing to Martha Blount after leaving her at Mapledurham so his mood may not have been appreciative.

From Stonor the road leads gently through the hills to meet the A 423 a mile and a half before Henley (and so to the limit of this section); but a slight detour along the lane marked 'Bixbottom' is worth the making. Bix is one of those villages which—to use the archaeologists' word—has migrated; it is now a bright little place alongside the Henley–Wallingford road. Originally Bix—the name comes from the box-trees which still grow hereabouts—lay in a bottom more than a mile to the north with its grazing land up at

Maidensgrove. A little-used lane leads beyond Little Bixbottom Farm to the site of the former village. Only the ruin of the church is left, half-hidden in a copse and with ivy splitting its walls. It was obviously built in Norman times; it has a plain door-arch and one small, round-headed window of about 1100. Somewhere nearby, perhaps under the thriving nettles, there must be traces of the former houses. It would be interesting to know when and why the original village died. Was Bix one of those villages which, when the Black Death ravaged the country in 1349, was abandoned by its few survivors, or were the villagers lured away to the present main-road site by the hope of business from passers-by?

Another route from Icknield through this area begins at Wat-lington. After crossing the Upper Icknield, it climbs up Watlington Hill to Christmas Common which is said to owe its name to an incident in the Civil War. The Parliamentarians were holding Wat-lington, the Royalists were defending the ridge; at Christmas 1643, the story tells, both sides were moved to mark the season of goodwill with a temporary truce, and they met on this spot.

From Christmas Common an easterly lane leads to Northend, another rather scattered ridge-top hamlet with its pond, before descending through beechwoods to Turville—and if the visitor is surprised at so French-seeming a name in so obviously English a setting, he should blame the Normans' inability to pronounce the Saxon 'Thyri-feld', Thyri's field.

At first glance Turville looks an obvious candidate for inclusion in 'Beautiful Britain' calendars. The houses, of flint, brick and half-timbering, are grouped along two sides of the triangular green; on the other side, backed by larch trees, stands the squat-towered church. Behind rise the hills on one of which stands a windmill (minus its sails but still undeniably once a windmill) to give an 'olde worlde' touch. It is not surprising that Nikolaus Pevsner is moved to depart from his somewhat terse summaries to mention that Turville 'is very pretty by the church', or that, some twenty years ago, the village provided the background to a sentimental and improbably bucolic film. And yet those who have not actually been there are almost unaware that it exists.

In Turville it is the total effect that counts. The individual cottages and houses are pleasant in themselves and many must be nearing three hundred years old—which is in fact older than much of the church fabric as seen from the village green, though the

latest reconstruction was discreet. But singly the buildings do not add up to the village as a whole. It is the grouping of the cottages, some standing forward, some slightly withdrawn, and the contrasts between their colours—some warmly red, some glinting with knapped flint, some black-and-white—and the hills' greennesses rising up behind all, that make Turville.

It is tempting to call Turville's a 'typical village church'; it has something to show of all that has happened to it. The building was begun before 1100—indeed the font is pre-Conquest, which hints that the Norman lord-of-the-manor destroyed an even earlier church to build his own. Of the Norman building, however, only the blocked north door and the ghost of a former round-headed window survive. The tower appears to date from the fourteenth century (as does one of the windows) but was in 1502 reported as being in 'a ruinous condition'; a century later we know it had been rebuilt, probably somewhat shorter than it originally was. But oddly the top foot or so is of brick and of rather poor workmanship—which suggests a somewhat hasty completion. And that, in turn, suggests that all may not have been well in Turville.

There is a possible clue to the apparently hasty finish to Turville's tower in one of the south windows of the church. A small portion of old glass shows the arms of Mary Tudor—but it is only a half-shield, the other half missing. That missing half would have shown, as is a matter of course, the arms of her husband, Philip of Spain, for whom Mary faced a rebellion which, had it been delayed a year or two, might have driven her from the throne. It looks as if Turville church was being restored and its tower rebuilt during those dangerous mid-Tudor decades when, after Henry VIII's break with Rome and his establishing of the Church of England, first young Edward VI's regents tried to make the whole country Protestant and then Mary tried to force it back again to Rome. Who in such uncertain and often dangerous years would spend more than necessary on the partly rebuilt tower of an insignificant village church? The safest course would have been to finish it off somehow—brick would have been cheaper than stone carted from far away—in order to avoid a charge of not having the building ready for whatever variety of church service should be demanded.

One gets the impression that through these centuries Turville must have been rather a poor place. There is in the church no hint of a lord of the manor at least maintaining it as his family mausoleum until 1733, when the north aisle was added as a chapel for the

Perry family, descended from the Dudleys and the Sidneys of Elizabeth's time.

Attractive though Turville is, from time to time a shadow lies over the place, a shadow created more by newspaper reporters hard up for a story than by reality. It concerns the stone coffin, probably of thirteenth-century date, which now stands in the tower. The story as often repeated goes like this: during the restoration of 1900 the coffin, which had been hidden under the chancel floor, was accidentally opened and was found to contain not the expected remains of a priest of the thirteenth century, but a much more recent skeleton; the skeleton was that of a woman, and there was a bullet hole in her skull. Such a find prompted much gruesome speculation which collected appropriate embroidery. The probable explanation is much less sensational. As a recent vicar has explained in his notes on the church, in medieval times and later it was quite usual, when a churchyard had become over-populated, for old graves to be re-opened for fresh interments. The remains discovered during the necessary digging were often placed anywhere available (in some old churches there was a chute from graveyard to crypt for the purpose). As Turville's thirteenth-century coffin, long embedded in the chancel floor, was by the sixteen-hundreds—the age of the female skeleton—too large for what was left of its original occupant, what would have been more suitable than that a more recent skeleton, unearthed in a search for new burial space in the churchyard, should be placed in it? (Incidentally, the stone coffin, when opened, was found to contain besides the two skeletons, an assortment of unattached bones; and, in case the absence of any reference to a wooden coffin should be remarked, it was customary during the seventeenth century to bury the more humble dead in their shrouds which, by law, had to be of wool in order to foster wool production.) It is not unlikely that at some point in the process, perhaps in the initial digging in the churchyard, the skeleton was damaged; a chance blow with a pick probably produced the 'bullet hole'. The raising of the chancel floor in a subsequent restoration made possible an added sinister touch to the story when, in 1900, the coffin was 'found hidden'.

It is time to leave Turville. Only a mile to the east, in another hollow in the hills, lies Fingest.

Of all the villages so far mentioned, Fingest is the best known beyond its immediate neighbourhood. Its Norman church with its surprisingly lofty tower, also Norman, seems to have found its way

into half the books dealing with the history of architecture in Britain, and for the less architecturally inclined, it certainly makes a picture against its background of steep, wood-topped hills. But there are other buildings in Fingest: some pleasantly red cottages and, facing the church, the Chequers. Of red brick diapered with purple, the inn's neat, almost precise front is late Stuart in date and is in its way as good an example of its time as Fingest's more famous building. Internally, though modified to present-day needs, many original features have been kept.

Fingest's church like Turville's suggests by its absence of large monuments that no local land-owning family used it as a mausoleum (and so, from time to time, altered or added to the original structure); but unlike Turville's the Norman builders of Fingest did their work well. The yard-thick walls have been plastered, later windows have allowed more light, and the tower has been reroofed, at some time in the sixteenth century probably, with twin brick gables; but otherwise the church remains very Norman and so narrow that five paces from the door you stub your toe on the opposite wall. The chancel is, strictly, of about 1230 but has the same simplicity. There is indeed very little in the place that detracts from the feeling of great age; even the Royal Arms is something of a rarity, being not of one of the Georges but those of Queen Anne.

If the visitor has the time, a short way along the street northwards from the church gate is the village pound, an iron replacement of about 1760. It is not a work of art but an oddity worth noting. From medieval times until a century or so ago nearly every village had its pound in which animals found straying were kept until their owner paid the fine to cover any damage they had done. Somehow pounds, unlike lych-gates and stocks, have never caught the public eye to become fashionable 'by-gones' and few are now left.

From Fingest a lane winds uphill to the outskirts of High Wycombe; but the visitor can turn back a short way and take the lane that leads south to Hambleden. On the way he will pass through Skirmett, a hamlet of brick and flint with a few modern 'Georgian' houses that blend well; it is more remarkable for its name than its appearance. Unexpectedly Skirmett and Fingest mean much the same. Fingest or more accurately 'Tinge-hurst', is Anglo-Saxon for 'wooded hill of Assembly'; Skirmett is Danish for 'Shire-meeting-place'. What the Danes were doing there one can only guess. Though in Alfred's time this land may have been fought over, the Danish

invaders scarcely occupied it for long enough to have set up the contemporary form of local government implied by Skirmett's name. More probably it was under Canute that the humble hamlet achieved, if only briefly, its distinction.

Hambleden down the valley is a compact village with its houses standing close around the churchyard. Though many of them appear of fairly recent date, the traditional flint, with brick outlines and tile roofs, has been used. The general effect is warm and trim, though perhaps not sentimental enough to have made Hambleden a recognised 'pretty village'. The church is rather large for the place and appreciation of it must depend on one's feelings about Victorian restorers. No doubt but for them many old churches would by now have become sorry ruins; and in Hambleden's church they have refurbished much of the fourteenth-century work. (Little of the earlier Norman church apparently survived to Victorian times, the building having been remodelled between 1230 and 1340 and the tower rebuilt in 1721.) The building now is perhaps a little too good to be true. In fifty or so years' time, perhaps, when the window tracery is not so obviously an imitation of the earlier work, the church will again seem the one known to the locals of medieval times.

Within a mile south of Hambleden the hills open out as the road approaches the Thames and the Henley–Marlow road (A 4155). At the junction is Mill End with its mill, mill-house and a farm or two, and beyond, its weirs and lock, a spot well known to those who enjoy the Thames. On the narrow lowland the Romans built a villa on top of an Iron Age settlement; excavations have revealed a mosaic floor, several fourth-century coins, fourteen furnaces, and nearly one hundred infant burials which to archaeologists suggest a crude method of population control.

A melancholy note to end on: so perhaps, before taking the homeward road, a glance at Medmenham two miles east along the Marlow road might be welcomed. Wedged between the river and a sharp hill capped with an Iron Age fort, Medmenham attracts visitors for varying reasons. Some are drawn by the long, low Dog and Badger opposite the church and claiming the date 1390 A.D.— a little optimistic perhaps when applied to the present fabric but less so than many allegedly ancient pubs. For others Medmenham is States House, hidden in the beechwoods, where Sir Basil Liddell Hart lived. The military philosopher and strategist of the inter-war years who early saw the shape of the war-to-come, he tried in a

dozen books and hundreds of press articles to persuade the British government to heed his logic but instead—such are the dangers of publication—became for the German High Command 'the creator of the theory of the conduct of mechanical war' and so prompted the Panzer forces and the 'Blitzkrieg'. This led some during the thirties, that decade of 'mental lassitude and moral fecklessness', to regard him as a war-monger, a wholly unjust assumption; he was, rather, one who came to accept the old maxim: 'let him who desires peace prepare for war', and he strove to awaken both government and people to the dangers in apparent indifference to the gathering storm. Since the war he has come to be regarded by some as a prophet—which is perhaps not wholly just to the inter-war governments who by hindsight heeded him too little and too late but had at the time to cope with reluctant public opinion as well as their own credulity. The last word has not yet been written on that momentous decade; but though Liddell Hart must be regarded as one of its outstanding figures—and also as a masterly historian of the world wars—history surely will make of him more than a voice crying in the wilderness as many of us too often regarded him.

This gentle man of war now lies at peace in Medmenham churchyard alongside which a lane leads down to Medmenham Abbey with its gardens reaching to the water's edge. Of thirteenth-century Cistercian foundation, the abbey was transformed into a country mansion after the Reformation, all but rebuilt in an eighteenth-century imitation of Gothic—and was rented by Sir Francis Dashwood of whose so-called 'Hell-Fire Club' more will be said when visiting West Wycombe—and thoroughly remodelled again in 1898, so that little of the Tudor house and less of the medieval monastery remains. But if the visitor, peering through the trees by the ferry-stage, likes to imagine that the cloisters he is seeing are those the monks walked, or that the house behind once knew the orgies of eighteenth-century rakes, it would perhaps be unkind to act the purist.

FIVE

From the Oxford Road to the Risborough Gap

The Oxford Road, A 40, looks on the ground and on the map like a recent work. From High Wycombe it takes a gently curving way up a long bottom; and, having attained nearly 800 feet—just where it crosses the ridge-top route—the descent is cut into the escarpment as if no thought had been given in advance as to how the road was going to reach the plain. This is neither the behaviour of a road which had grown up through millennia of serving as a link between settlements nor the product of a military mind. And its destination, Oxford, is for all its antiquity in our eyes of medieval origin. The peoples of prehistory used its marsh-protected site only intermittently, and the Romans ignored it.

By contrast the next major road through the Chilterns, that linking High Wycombe and Thame, follows a course nearly as ancient as Icknield. The modern road is in fact not on the original line, but the Risborough gap and the valley of the Wye leading to the Thames was, as has been mentioned, used from Neolithic times onwards.

Between the two main roads the Icknield Way becomes officially doubled. Just where the Oxford Road levels after its winding descent through the beechwoods of Aston Hill, the Upper Icknield crosses it. It is still a green lane and, after the incessant traffic of the main road, still quiet and easy-going—though as it approaches Chinnor, halfway to Risborough, it has to negotiate an extensive cement works. This stretch, however, the walker can easily avoid by taking the parallel Lower Icknield Way.

Whatever its most southerly starting-point the Lower Icknield is indisputably north of the Oxford Road. The 'Viatores' confirm its Roman use, but its gently curving way across a landscape of cornfields hints that it might have originated before the days of align-

66

13. *Church Lane, West Wycombe*

VILLAGE
STREETS

corner of Braughing

15. *Village pond at Aldbury*

THE ESSENTIAL WATER

16. *Hill-top pond at Northend, Turville*

ments. It is very rural. Only a few paces from the main road and a walker has for company only his own thoughts, the yellow-hammers in the sparse hedges or here and there a flock of pigeons or rooks, and across the undulating fields an occasional glimpse of a village backed by the line of the hills until Chinnor comes in sight. There the Lower Icknield becomes a road, but those who prefer to walk can leave the village on its southerly and pleasanter side to find the Upper Way, now free of the cement works, skirting the escarpment rich with trees ... which route will lead through the wood below Wain Hill to Princes Risborough (though the last mile or so, a lane, looks as if the Way was tidied up a bit when the Enclosure Commissioners did their job).

For the motoring traveller there is the road running between the Ways and about a half-mile from each; after Chinnor it takes over the Lower Icknield. The villages hereabouts, true to Icknield custom, lie between the Ways.

From the Oxford Road the first village is Aston Rowant. It is rather an odd little place: a few cottages about the church, mainly fourteenth century, well cared for and possessing some early glass; and then, at a distance, a large green with more houses spread around it. Here and there between the two little closes of new houses, many of them pleasant, satisfy planners' ideas of 'in filling', no doubt; they detract little from the green spaciousness of the village for many of the old trees and an occasional length of hedge have been permitted to remain.

Kingston Blount, a mile further on, is despite its impressive name only a hamlet, a rectangle of brief streets of mixed cottages and a farm or two. Its parish church is half a mile away at Crowell. Now little more than a dozen houses, an inn and a church, Crowell was once somewhat larger for the 1851 census records several families mostly engaged in agriculture and additionally three 'chair-turners', one 'chair-bottomer' and no less than sixteen lace-makers. These last would have been mostly housewives, but the fact that their occupation was recorded suggests that lacemaking was more than a casual, pin-money-making job. Originally established by Huguenot refugees further north around Newport Pagnell and Olney, it had spread southwards among the village women. During the first half of the seventeenth century 'lace schools' at which poor children were taught the craft were set up in many villages, and 'lacemen' travelled the country gathering the lace and marketing it. Though the craft appears to have died out further north early in the nineteenth

century, within living memory lacemakers were to be seen at many a cottage door in the Risborough neighbourhood, an indication of the remoteness of the area until the car arrived.

Crowell, so the brief history in its church records, was almost completely destroyed by fire in 1859. Looking at the place now, a few random cottages to which recent houses have been added, it is difficult to imagine the flames spreading from building to building. The little church, merely nave, chancel and bell-cote, was practically rebuilt in 1878. It looks still new; its restorer, however, did not impose his own variety of Victorian Gothic but retained as much as possible of the impression of the early fourteenth-century church. Nearby is Crowell's better-known building, the Catherine Wheel which, whether rebuilt or not, retains a village-inn atmosphere. It is little more than a cottage; for its bar there is a lean-to at the back said to have been formerly the sleeping quarters (with the earthen floor for a bed if the report is true) for the drovers who until the middle of the last century still used the Icknield route when bringing beef from the West Country to the markets of the corn-producing eastern counties. The inn also claims that John Bunyan, between his spells in gaol, stayed at the Catherine Wheel and entertained the locals on a flute which, when in prison, he hid by camouflaging it as a chair stretcher—though how he came to be so far from his native Bedford need not trouble the visitor as he takes his refreshment.

Crowell has a second literary link, with Bunyan's contemporary Milton. It was the birthplace of Thomas Ellwood, a personal friend of Milton for whom he rented the well-known cottage in Chalfont St Giles as a refuge from plague-stricken London. A prominent Quaker who suffered imprisonment and near-starvation for his convictions, Ellwood also suggested to Milton one of his greater poems. The story tells that having read the manuscript of *Paradise Lost*, he commented to the poet: 'Thou hast said much of Paradise Lost, but what hast thou to say of Paradise Found?' The question lodged in Milton's mind and as he later told Ellwood prompted him to write *Paradise Regained*.

Chinnor, whose main street ends at a T-junction on the Lower Icknield, is larger but not more attractive. It is not helped by the proximity of the cement works, no doubt an economic necessity but hardly an attraction. There are a few pleasant houses, new and oldish, but the village wears a slightly forlorn look. It has a long history—Iron-Agers lived there, the Romans built at least one size-

able house and, much later, the Royalists and Parliamentarians fought a lively and bloody skirmish for the place—and yet, apart from its church it has little to show.

The church was originally Norman, as the blocked north door-way shows; but early in the fourteenth century Chinnor must have been prosperous enough to undertake an almost complete rebuild-ing. The church is now a good example of its time, and almost complete village churches of what the ecclesiologist calls 'Early Decorated' are not readily to be found. Decoration in the form of leaf-shapes around the capitals, of tracery in windows, of figures and gargoyles, was coming in during the 1320s when Chinnor church was being rebuilt; and they are still there to see, together with two remarkable windows of fourteenth-century glass, gentler in colour and subtler in feeling than the more usual Victorian glass. And it has collected no less than thirteen brasses dating from 1325 to 1514. It also has a collection of eighteenth-century pictures about which it is a little difficult to be enthusiastic. It is unjust to question their presence; the rector of a village church could not often lay down how his church should be adorned and as the pictures were probably the work of James Thornhill, said to be the first English painter to be knighted (overlooking apparently Van Dyck), to decline them would have appeared ungracious; or perhaps their rather inert appearance was favoured in the 1720s.

The next village, Bledlow, is a little beyond the cross cut in the chalk of the escarpment to which it has given its name: a landmark for every traveller through the neighbourhood. On the way there the traveller might feel tempted to turn aside at the sign 'Henton only'; the word 'only' suggests somewhere off the road, quiet and perhaps with its attractions as yet little known. If he does follow the wide-verged lane through the straggle of houses (and, though he may not notice it, past a moat which tells that in medieval times there was a homestead here) he will be rewarded by finding in the Eagle one of the most bucolic pubs left : a haphazard, unprofes-sional-looking mixture of timber, plaster, and bold brick chimney appearing almost to be struggling to support its thick thatch. It looks as if it has scarcely changed since Morland painted his village scenes showing cottages as they were in the 1790s before the wealthier and more progressive landlords had swept them away to build more sanitary, prim houses for their labourers and certainly before twentieth-century country-cottage-owners restored the larger of the survivors.

On to Bledlow which stands on rising ground between the Lower Icknield and the Upper, here skirting round the last crest before the Risborough Gap opens the first easy way through the escarpment since the Thames valley.

Bledlow's original street runs parallel with Icknield. At one end is the Red Lions, low and inviting, and owing its plural name, it is said, to the presence formerly of two inns of the same name. Once a row of three cottages, its timbers inside show its seventeenth-century origin. Halfway along the street stands the church above a stream which has carved for itself a miniature gorge. And since the whole street runs across an outlier of the hills, between the cottages can be seen the vale of Aylesbury stretching away northwards or to the south the sharp rise of the escarpment with its wooded crest.

The church, built a decade or two before Chinnor's was rebuilt and altered little since, was like many another medieval church decorated with wall paintings. Though it is still possible to trace how extensive they once were, time has treated the paintings harshly. It has, however, been kinder to the gargoyles round the tower, a mixed set appearing from the ground almost complete and giving, as gargoyles often do, a glimpse into the strange, half-literal, half-fantasy world of the medieval sculptor.

Bledlow also had a distinctive if not distinguished incumbent in Timothy Hall, installed in 1674. When in 1687 James II published his unwelcome Declaration of Indulgence—a belated attempt to win popular support—Hall was one of the few clergymen who read the royal order to their congregation. (Most ignored it but at least one other complied with the King's wishes—after first asking his congregation to leave.) The widespread and hostile reaction was an expression of the opposition James had aroused and, as the textbooks reminded us, led to the Glorious and/or Bloodless Revolution of 1688. Timothy Hall benefited only very briefly from his obsequious act. When he was rewarded with the bishopric of Oxford we are told that 'the Dean and Canons ... refused to install him, the gentry to meet him, the Vice-Chancellor and Heads to take any notice of him'. History has been no less unkind: he 'had no merit but that of reading the king's declaration' is the *Dictionary of National Biography*'s epitaph.

Bledlow Cross, white against the green of the escarpment, has a rather larger companion at Whiteleaf, the first village on the other side of the Risborough gap. In the past these two crosses

70

prompted much argument; they were variously dated from pre-Christian times to the eighteenth century, and their purpose guessed at from mystical signs to mere guides to travellers. The first firm date is 1742, the publication date of a book called *Further Observations upon the White Horse and other Antiquities in Berkshire*; the author, Francis Wise, Radcliffe Librarian, interpreting Berkshire somewhat widely, includes an illustration of Whiteleaf Cross which he assumes to be ancient. Though he mentions an earthwork at Bledlow, he does not mention its Cross. The first written reference to Bledlow's Cross is more recent, but it also makes it clear that there may have been a Bledlow Cross much earlier. The reference occurs in a letter in an early number of *Records of Buckinghamshire*; the writer tells that his father, who owned the estate on which the Cross was situated, found it in 1802 by 'accidentally walking over it', and subsequently had its grass covering cleared away. It seems that the passer-by can, if he wishes, assert an earlier date without risk of contradiction.

It would be fitting for Bledlow Cross to be of ancient workmanship. If ever there were a few square miles of countryside which should cause an imaginative traveller to recall Byron's 'Where'er we tread, 'tis haunted, holy ground', it is the Bledlow neighbourhood. There where the Upper Icknield negotiates the first gap in the chalk escarpment north of the Thames have been found signs of human habitation from the earliest times: Old Stone-Agers' tools and Neolithic weapons on the lower land, Bronze Age barrows on the hill-tops and reaching along the gap to the mysterious Lodge Hill, Iron Age habitation sites, a Roman villa, sundry as yet unclassified Roman buildings and a Romano-British village site. Nor should we assume these to be a series of local, self-sufficient communities; even in Neolithic times there was trading between settlements far apart as is evidenced by a polished stone axe found in the Cop at Bledlow made from stone from Cornwall while another found at nearby Whiteleaf originated in Westmorland. And all this before a Saxon leader named Bledda appeared on the scene to name the place after his hill—or was the 'hlaw', which can mean mound as well as hill, one of the barrows above Bledlow which pre-Christian Saxons used for their interments, including perhaps that of Bledda himself?

If this sequence of habitation fails to provide enough haunting for the visitor, if such remote peoples to whom we shall probably never be able to give much more than a dim reality have failed

to set his imagination to work, perhaps the next item of Bledlow's long history will help. Some 900 years ago Bledlow's inhabitants beheld (or more probably hid from) a body of passers-by whom we can, thanks to contemporary chronicles, modern research and the Bayeux tapestry, visualise much more clearly.

It is now over seventy years since F. H. Baring, studying Domesday Book, noticed that the recorded 'values' of a string of villages in the Southeast had abruptly diminished between the death of Edward the Confessor in January 1066 and early 1067 when they were awarded to their new Norman lords. Baring plotted these shrunken-valued villages on the map and discovered that they occupied a fairly narrow strip of country making a roughly S-shaped route from the Hastings–Dover neighbourhood to near Hertford. Along the course Baring noticed were offshoots—such as one to Southwark which the chroniclers had said a contingent of William's victorious army visited, and another towards Winchester where Edward's widowed queen had accepted William's victory to forestall an attack on the city. Baring had, after a gap of over eight hundred years, discovered the route by which the Norman Conqueror had approached London after the Battle of Hastings; and a circuitous route it was while he hoped that the Saxon Witenagemot in London would make up their minds to accept him as King without first compelling him to attack the city. On their way the Normans had, as is ever the custom with invading armies, gathered their supplies en route and, as the recorded loss of production shows, were not squeamish about encouraging occupants reluctant to hand over their stock and stores with some exemplary destruction. Baring had also discovered that 'Beorcham' where, according to the chroniclers, William finally received the submission of London, was not Great Berkhamsted, as had long been assumed, but Little Berkhamsted near Hertford; for it was there that the Norman route ended.

More recently Charles H. Lemmon, in his contribution to *The Norman Conquest: its setting and impact*, published in 1966 to mark the ninth centenary of the Battle of Hastings, has filled in some of Baring's outline. Studying again the despoiled villages plotted by Baring, Lemmon has discovered that groups of villages at about twenty-five mile intervals suffered more heavily than others along the route. These he deduced marked the halting-places of the main force, probably of at least two days' duration since, as Lemmon says, 'the necessity for catching, killing, dressing, cooking

and eating animals, also for collecting corn for grinding and making bread, would make daily marching impossible'.

To follow Baring's and Lemmon's discoveries all the way from Hastings would go far beyond the Chiltern region. For the present it is enough to note that the Chiltern area appears to have been approached from two directions. The main army—Lemmon assumes the cavalry—which had gone as far westwards as to threaten Winchester, approached the Thames about Dorchester and Wallingford, probably using both crossing places. Wallingford was the walled 'burh' which served as a barracks for the Saxon professional 'house-carls'—the earthen banks are still to be seen —and William would certainly have left there a force sufficient to hold it. Nearby Dorchester suffered some spoliation. To the southeast, Basildon and Aston also suffered and both authorities suggest that a secondary force, possibly mainly of infantry and following a roughly parallel course, crossed the river about Goring. Thereafter, with the annoying habit of ancient records, there is a gap while the forces apparently crossed the huge manor of Bensington (now Benson) and the exact route cannot be plotted. The Domesday record of Thame suggests that it was visited but did not suffer heavily—probably it saw the passage but not a prolonged stop of the main force making its way towards the Chiltern escarpment to link up with the secondary force that was moving northwards along Icknield.

The two forces appear to have met at Bledlow. The village— it cannot have been a large place—suffered heavily; nearby Risborough also suffered, proportionately less though the Domesday figures suggest that it was smaller; and so too did the villages on northwards as William, apparently taking little heed of the possibility of an attack via the Risborough gap, moved off towards the Roman road between Tring and Aylesbury. Indeed the figures of spoliation hereabouts suggest that either the Norman forces spent a day or two spread out in the villages along Icknield or they made their way very leisurely, finding time to inflict what must have been for such insignificant places heavy damage.

As if the Bledlow neighbourhood had not seen enough of history, nearby—between it and Risborough—are traces not of the Normans' passing but of the half-forgotten changes that were to come to some villages during medieval times. About halfway between the two Icknield Ways as they leave Bledlow is Horsenden; it is what archaeologists have in recent years come to call a 'lost

village'. Down a lane that peters out in the flat land in the centre of the Risborough gap, Horsenden is now only half a dozen recent houses and a fragment of what must have been a sizeable village church. Now only the original chancel serves the local needs; a tower built in 1765 stands where once the nave began. It is a quiet, half-forgotten place—though those who venture to it will be rewarded with the sight of an almost toy-like wooden dove-cote, probably built when Horsenden was still a village.

What interests archaeologists about such a place, however, is not what is now but what was. Recently many such villages have been discovered, once places of local importance, now little more than a farm or two, the remains of an ancient church, perhaps —as near Horsenden—a moat that once surrounded a medieval homestead, and sometimes unevennesses in the ground hinting of former house-sites. Expert curiosity is stirred: what made the village 'disappear'? It is no longer sufficient to say 'Black Death' or 'Plague' and leave it at that. Recent investigation of some such sites has yielded other reasons for their being abandoned. Sometimes economic factors have been the suspected cause: a decline in the price of grain, for example, could cause a landlord to turn his estate over to the more profitable wool-producing sheep; or the early attempts at enclosure, practised from about 1500 onwards by go-ahead landowners who were beginning to find advantages in farming arable land not in the ancient open fields but in smaller, more compact units, and so persuaded, urged or drove their villagers away—and provoked the wrath of Cardinal Wolsey among others and sometimes found themselves facing him in court to answer for their high-handed actions. Or perhaps it may have been lordly pride demanding that the local great house should be surrounded by a park worthy of its newly rich owner—and humble villagers' cottages, of wood and mud often, could have no place alongside the vistas avenued from his lordship's windows or among the copses cunningly placed to improve his lordship's view. Or perhaps it was merely that the siting had been a mistake, that the original village had been on land that had, perhaps due to unwise farming, gradually become exhausted. Only expert study can, sometimes, discover which of such causes has resulted in a particular village being 'lost', and so add to our understanding of the effects of economic and social changes on the lives of the humbler people of the countryside.

Princes Risborough, the last point on this stretch of Icknield,

is within a mile of Horsenden and backed by the sharply rising, wooded hill on which Whiteleaf Cross is cut. Though it is sited in an area that has seen so much and was itself the site of a Roman settlement, it has not very much to show. Once 'Great Risborough' —to distinguish it from adjoining Monks Risborough which back in about 1000 had been given to the monks of Canterbury—it has acquired its more distinctive name from one or other of a succession of princely owners, the best remembered being Edward, eldest son of Edward III, known to us as the Black Prince. Of the castle he or one of his predecessors built here only a few fragments of wall and a ditch remain. Near the church is The Mount, assumed to be of Saxon origin; near, too, is the town's oldest building, the Old Vicarage, a timber-framed fifteenth-century house, and the Manor House, built about 1700 of red brick to which, probably soon afterwards, a more imposing entrance with pediment and Doric pilasters was added. From the church runs Church Street with its pleasant mixture of sixteenth- and seventeenth-century houses. The rest of the place gives the impression that it began to grow from village into small town as first the mail-coaches and later the railway brought travellers to it and enabled it to serve as a centre for villages beyond Icknield. Its central feature is now its market hall, built in 1824. Its church was remodelled about a hundred years ago, and was given its tower as recently as 1908, since when the railway and the car have brought more people and so encouraged more building around it, giving the town an even more recent appearance.

The seven miles or so of Icknield between the Oxford Road and Risborough skirts a section of the Chilterns curiously fragmented by its ridges. On the crest stretch beechwoods; behind them, tilting towards High Wycombe are several sharp ridges separated by deep bottoms with hamlets scattered about them but scarcely a recognisable village.

A good approach to this area is to take the lane that leads southwards from the end of Chinnor's street and then as it climbs abruptly up to the ridge, take the lane branching off southwestwards at a very sharp bend. This by-way climbs to the top of Crowell Hill and then turns along a ridge to Andridge Common to give uncluttered views of the twisting bottoms of Radnage parish. Radnage is said once to have been a village standing just below its church; now it is half a dozen hamlets, with pleasant

cottages and farms along them and with such names as 'The City', 'Town End', and 'Bennett End' (where above a brick-and-timber farm stands the Three Horseshoes, which fittingly is ancient and attractive).

Radnage church, on a hillside to the north of the hamlets it serves, is often rather cursorily treated by the guide-books: it consists only of nave, tower and chancel of early thirteenth-century date, and there are traces of wall-paintings—some such summary has often to do, and may suffice for those who look for almost cathedral splendour in every ancient church. Such a description overlooks the essence of Radnage church; it was—and still is— the church of a small rural community, and was raised not by a rich monastery or by some prosperous fifteenth-century wool-merchant to the glory of God and his own family, but probably largely by the locals working, we must assume, under a master craftsman knowledgeable in contemporary building ideas; and it was built as their church. No doubt then—probably soon after 1200—it was the pride of the place; its pointed chancel arches (with the tower between them) and the slim lancet windows above the altar, were then very modern. And, built at a time when renewed religious fervour was tending to move away from the decoration of the later Norman churches—the elaborate mouldings which we admire —Radnage church is appropriately plain. And so, essentially, it has remained ever since—though about a hundred years after its building, larger windows allowed more light into the nave, and the roof had to be replaced, that of the chancel apparently in the fourteenth century, the nave roof about a century later. Like many another Chiltern church—like Checkendon, for example, or Ipsden —it may be architecturally humble and is certainly unpretentious; but it is unmistakably the product of its time and of the local people who lived at that time.

Nearby is the red-brick, eighteenth-century Old Vicarage, now a private house (and very carefully restored). It appears very large for such a village as Radnage—and that, too, is in keeping. In the eighteenth century the Church often offered a rich and respected living for the younger sons of gentlemen; it also enabled them to be regarded as near equals of the local squirearchy. The earlier priest's house, often little better than those of his parishioners, would never have suited such a way of living; the local vicarage had to be if not the great house of the village at least impressive enough to enable its occupant to join the local gentry at the meet or at

the county ball, as well as delivering to them an hour-long sermon on Sundays.

From Radnage a winding lane leads up to Stokenchurch high on the Chiltern crest and, like Radnage, a place that seldom gets much notice in the travel books—with more justification. Stokenchurch should be an attractive place; it is spread around three different greens with good trees on them; it has a church that was once Norman, and a mixture of houses of different periods; and yet the effect is disappointing. It suggests not the haphazardness gathered through changing centuries, but rather prolonged indifference. Perhaps now that the main road traffic by-passes it along the motorway it will take more pride in its appearance and, indeed, some of the newer streets of houses are trim and pleasant. So could the whole place be, though it is probably too much to hope that one day the work of the Victorian restorers of its church—a meagre, muddle-headed lot they must have been—will be guided back to something nearer to what once was.

Another route into the hills leads southwards from Bledlow; but the walker gets the best of it. He can leave the lane as it begins to climb towards Bledlow Ridge and follow the ancient route, a branch from the Upper Icknield Way and nearly as old, over Lodge Hill. This strange fragment of upland rises curiously apart from the ridges hereabouts, with trees clinging to one side, leaving the summit almost bare. And as the walker may notice it is composed of an unexpectedly dark, sandy soil. No doubt a geologist will tell that it is a surviving fragment of a glacial moraine or the random result of an inundation; but to the early peoples who from Icknield found their way to Lodge Hill that oddly sandy soil offered easy cultivation. And others following them found the same attraction—and probably found that so light a soil was soon exhausted. Neolithic tools, fragments of Bronze Age pottery and of Iron Age ware too, have been found where rabbits or badgers have burrowed; slight circular hollows suggest hut sites and several burial mounds have been traced, two of which still survive at the northern edge of the hill. And the ancient route leads on southeastwards along the ridge, to pass through the woods that now cover what was, in medieval times, the village of Averingdon, to end up at an Iron Age fort encircling what was Averingdon's church but has now become West Wycombe's. It is a footpath as haunted as many a stretch of Icknield, and giving fine views, too.

The motorist can follow a roughly parallel route along the lane that climbs up to Bledlow Ridge and slopes down at its south-easterly end into West Wycombe village; but he may be a little disappointed on the way. Bledlow Ridge sounds as if it, too, will offer wide views; it does—but mostly to the houses that, in the inter-war years, were built along it. Only at each end of the ridge does the motorist get much visual benefit.

West Wycombe means different things to different visitors. For those who know the place only from driving along the old Oxford Road its much photographed street is perhaps unequalled. For those who look further into West Wycombe, there are sights about which perhaps the fairest comment was that of one of the boys who unlock the church door: 'It's about fifty-fifty,' he said. 'Some are very impressed, some can't stand it!'

Apart from the main street, West Wycombe is the creation of that odd eighteenth-century figure, Sir Francis Dashwood, later Lord Le Despencer, Member of Parliament, sometime Cabinet Minister, and according to popular belief founder of the notorious 'Hell-Fire Club'. First at Medmenham Abbey on the Thames and later in caves at West Wycombe and even in the giant ball which surmounts the church tower, this Club, it is said, held profane and obscene orgies which shocked the not-easily-shockable eighteenth-century society and, later, were whispered about with satisfying horror by those Victorians who came to hear of the alleged goings-on. For the benefit of today's visitors, there are waxwork models in eighteenth-century costume and posed to prompt appropriate feelings while a tape-recording tells the story.

As readers of Betty Kemp's thorough biography, *Sir Francis Dashwood: an Eighteenth Century Independent,* will know, the story of the 'Hell-Fire Club' has little basis in fact. Dashwood, like many another eighteenth-century gentleman, not infrequently entertained his friends at his country houses: here at West Wycombe and also at Medmenham Abbey which he rented. Dashwood was a much-travelled man with an interest in the arts and especially in classical architecture, then very much in vogue among the well-to-do. He formed a 'Society of Dilettanti' whose object was to encourage interest in the architecture of Greece and the Middle East; this was not so much an organisation as an occasional gathering of men with similar tastes. At times Dashwood and his friends entertained themselves in the then customary manner with slight performances which appear to have taken on a mock-religious air.

Portraits of several of the 'Society of Dilettanti' dressed in various costumes with Dashwood as a friar have survived. Dashwood appears to have been in fact genuinely interested in religious matters; he later joined with Benjamin Franklin (a most unlikely member of any 'Hell-Fire Club') in writing a simplified Prayer Book, and his tendencies were against the formalism of the Established Church and, probably more so, of Roman Catholicism. These informal parties would seem to have prompted Dashwood's enemies to dub him 'Saint Francis' and the Dilettanti Society 'Dashwood's Apostles'. The title 'Hell-Fire Club', then used for any gathering of rakes and roués, seems not at the time to have been applied to Dashwood's friends.

The clue to the disapproval that Dashwood aroused—and which, later, was embroidered into the stories now told—is to be found in the comments of Horace Walpole, the contemporary equivalent of a political commentator:

> He and some of his friends had hired the ruins of Medmenham Abbey, near Marlow, and refitted it in a conventual style.... Their follies would have escaped the eye of the public, if Lord Bute from this seminary of piety and wisdom had not selected a Chancellor of the Exchequer. But politics had no sooner infused themselves among these rosy anchorites, than dissensions were kindled, and a false brother arose, who ... exposed the good Prior in order to ridicule him as Minister of the Finances.

Lord Bute was the Prime Minister of the day whom the young and idealistic George III had chosen to end the Seven Years' War with France; Sir Francis Dashwood, as his Chancellor of the Exchequer, had the unpopular task of raising the taxation necessary to pay for Britain's costly victories. As neither Bute nor Dashwood was a member of the two political groupings of the day—'Whigs' and 'Tories' were hardly yet political parties—it is not surprising that they encountered opposition in both Houses, and in the eighteenth-century political opponents were not averse to muck-raking and even deliberate invention. Walpole himself at times spread a little opportune scandal; that his comments on the alleged activities of Dashwood and his friends were so mild is a clear indication that, as yet, little scandalous had occurred.

Another readily remembered opponent of the government of the day was John Wilkes who, having attacked the King personally

in his newspaper *The North Briton*, judged it necessary to spend a few years in France to escape a charge of seditious libel. (His subsequent return and the fiasco of the Middlesex elections which made him appear the champion of popular liberties is a later part of his story.) Wilkes, hostile to any member of His Majesty's government, told vaguely of 'English Eleusinian Mysteries' practised by the Chancellor of the Exchequer and his friends at Medmenham Abbey; Wilkes's associate, Charles Churchill, wrote—also somewhat vaguely—of black magic, mock-religious ceremonies, and orgies there without giving any source for his assertions. At about the same time a Charles Johnstone wrote a picaresque novel, *Chrysal, or the Adventures of a Guinea*, in which he included descriptions of the activities of 'a person of flighty imagination' on an island retreat where in 'a building on the mode of monasteries ... there was not a vice ... for practising which he did not make provision'. Whether Johnstone was trying to implicate Dashwood and his Society of Dilettanti or merely indulging his own rather lurid imagination is far from sure. The coincidence of this novel with the other hints would seem to have started off the stories of the so-called 'Hell-Fire Club' and so led to the tableaux at West Wycombe—in one of which appears John Wilkes, an unlikely member of Dashwood's circle who is incidentally known to have visited Medmenham only once, on 21 July 1762.

Whatever may be assumed or guessed about Dashwood's private life, it is his interest in architecture that should bring the visitor to West Wycombe, for it was there that he gave lasting expression to the ideas he and his friends had collected as a result of many trips to Greece and beyond. He had inherited a house already fifty years old and set about with the formal gardens of an earlier fashion. Beyond the gardens stretched a park, probably mainly farming land, and on the ridge above the village stood a medieval church. In 1750 Dashwood set about remodelling it all.

He did it thoroughly. He employed several of the best-known architects of the day, he brought over noted Italian artists to undertake the internal decoration, he used contemporary gardening experts to lay out the estate. He transformed the house, the gardens, the surroundings and the church. To the house Dashwood added its colonnaded exterior and reconstructed and redecorated the interior; it was refashioned on the lines of Palladio's Palazzo Chiericati, near Venice. The earlier formality of the garden was replaced by cunningly informal landscaping and embellished with summer-

houses, follies, and 'temples'. Of the medieval church he left only the lower stages of the tower, and that he surmounted with a huge golden ball suggested, it is said, by that on the Customs Building at Venice, and capable of seating, inside, seven or eight people. The medieval nave, chancel and aisles gave way to what a contemporary called 'a very superb Egyptian Hall'; it is said to be based on the Temple of the Sun at Palmyra, and its ceiling, appropriately painted, is supported on porphyry columns embellished with stucco garlands. The whole, including the chancel, is paved with marble. Certainly Dashwood did not skimp things—though the visitor who does not find the result to his taste in church architecture can, perhaps, find relief in memorial reading: a later Dashwood was 'a dutiful Son, an affectionate Brother and a tender Husband; he married Elizabeth Callander, and died...' It could have been more gallantly phrased.

As a final gesture—though in fact he spent the last few years of his life still making further improvements—Dashwood created the mausoleum, said to have been based on Constantine's Arch at Rome. It is formed by a darkly flint wall enclosing a hexagonal, unroofed space. Through its screens can be seen monuments to three Dashwood ladies. These are often said to have been three of Dashwood's four wives. As two of the ladies, both named Mary Dashwood, died when he was two years old and eleven respectively, such a slipshod assumption credits him with a precocity that even the most ardent believer in the 'Hell-Fire Club' would boggle at. The ladies were his mother and one of his stepmothers; it was his father, another Sir Francis, who married four times. Dashwood's only wife, as Lady Le Despencer, also has a monument in the mausoleum.

This curious building was, for Dashwood, the focal point of his efforts. It was necessitated by his insistence that no one should be buried within his remodelled church. It stands just below the eastern end of the church so that to the visitor coming along the straight mile from High Wycombe it appears as the lower part of the church itself, the church tower with its golden ball seeming to rise out of it. To enhance the effect Dashwood had planted an avenue of appropriately dark pines (since replaced by chestnuts) leading up to the mausoleum.

The best summary of all that, architecturally speaking, is to be seen in Dashwood's West Wycombe can be found in Pevsner's *Buckinghamshire*. His comments are generally appreciative. But,

as has been hinted, there is now more to see than Pevsner records: the waxwork models of contemporary lace-makers and bodgers complete with accessories; the 'Bird World' and the 'Steam Age Collection', neither of which seems to have much connection with Dashwood or West Wycombe; and in the caves below the church—hollowed out at Dashwood's expense to provide flint for the road to High Wycombe, and a discouragingly chilly setting for orgies—are the tableaux of eighteenth-century figures, posed to suggest the alleged pastimes of the 'Hell-Fire Club' members. And if these are considered unsuitable for the children, there are donkey rides. . . .

The visitor has to make what he can of all this. If the architectural ideas of the eighteenth century do not appeal—if, for example, it is assumed that a church must have a medieval appearance—then much of what is to be seen will bring disappointment, perhaps disapproval. If the visitor comes expecting to be excited by the alleged immoralities of the 'Hell-Fire Club' he will need a very vivid imagination; the pornographic and sacrilegious symbols once whispered about have long since gone, if ever they existed. And if eighteenth-century Britain is viewed through visions only of its elegance, the recent attempts at showmanship may jar. But if the visitor approaches the many sights of West Wycombe merely curious to see how a wealthy eighteenth-century landowner gave expression to his architectural fancies then there is much for him. And if he recalls that, when Dashwood was transforming his estate to his liking, elsewhere in Britain the factories of the Industrial Revolution were imposing on their local people their own far from elegant forms of architecture, he may think it not unfitting that in our more egalitarian time far more people than Dashwood's era would have allowed can in their own way enjoy his handiwork.

And, whatever there is to be said for or against Dashwood's West Wycombe, there is the village itself, much of it built before his time. There is scarcely another street in the country to compare with it: the long double-row of cottages, inns and shops, a mixture of sixteenth century, seventeenth century and Georgian in which, as Pevsner says, 'except for the Methodist Church of 1894, nothing is visually wrong'. There is the timber-framed Church Loft, late medieval and formerly the village meeting-place (where is to be seen the village lock-up), and the George and Dragon, dated 1726, a somewhat bucolic attempt at early Georgian formality, and across the street, the Apple Orchard with its timber-and-brick overhang. There are 200-year-old brick cottages and more homely flint-walled

ones, and prim, flat-fronted houses, and here and there a bold gable. And in the brief side streets, particularly Church Lane, there are more. It is a place to loiter in—if the homeward-leading main road is not too insistent.

SIX

From the Risborough Gap to Akeman Street

It is perhaps not unfitting that for much of the next section of Icknield the Ways should be roads. They are traversing an area which was known to the Romans and all their successors; it has been peopled since history began, perhaps from prehistory. For the motorist it is therefore an area he can see from behind his car wheel—though since Icknield, even the Romanised Lower one, is as ever slightly winding and undulating he would be wise not to view the scenery too persistently while in motion.

For the walker, strictly speaking only the first mile of the Upper Way where it skirts Princes Risborough to the south is a path. From the hamlet of Whiteleaf there is only the road—unless the walker decides to abandon the strictly historical and accept the crest-following probability. Then he has some fine going ahead of him for the crest can be reached by a footpath across the golf links just south of the hamlet of Whiteleaf, and once up a selection of footpaths leads round the fort on Pulpit Hill—formerly Bull-pit Hill, which suggests that it may once have been used for the autumnal sacrificing-cum-preparing-winter-stores occasions that are believed to have been a feature of the pre-Roman tribal year and were certainly indulged in during Saxon times. (Hereabouts in late summer the almost bald slopes shimmer during sunny afternoons with hosts of minute butterflies.) The route turns more easterly above the Kimbles, Great and Little, to cross the hollow in which Chequers stands before climbing up again over Coombe Hill with its Boer War memorial to descend again to Wendover. From there a footpath starts below Boddington Hill with its Iron Age fort and skirts the lower edge of the wooded slope much as the Upper Icknield would have done—could this, rather than the road,

84

A 4011, be the Way? If the walker has little interest in viewing Halton R.A.F. Camp, he can on the other hand take the path up through Wendover Woods until, an energetic mile-and-a-half east of Wendover, there is a crest way which after crossing the quiet country about the hamlet of Hastoe descends to Tring. An alternative footpath from Wendover and a less arduous one is the towpath of the old canal, now much shrunken and the haunt of birds. It provides an easy and remote way, and beyond Drayton Beauchamp church offers a detour around Tring's two reservoirs, both now nature reserves. For those not historically intent and ready to accept in the interests of leisurely going a slight variation from Icknield it is to be recommended. In spring and early summer particularly it is half a dozen miles of delight.

For those who follow the Icknield route on from Princes Risborough the Lower Icknield, though a pleasant, easy road, has little to show until after the A 413. The villages hereabouts tend to be nearer the Upper Way. Monks Risborough, now almost a suburb of Princes, has retained a street of brick-and-timber cottages, some of them thatched, a church that dates from the fourteenth century, and a square, white-stone dovecote probably of Tudor date. Some hollows in the ground nearby are said to have been the site of medieval fishponds and suggest a monastery; but only a grange, a monastic farm belonging to Christchurch, Canterbury, seems to have provided the prefix 'Monks'.

The hamlet of Whiteleaf, as has been mentioned, is more than locally famous for its Cross, a somewhat larger version of that at Bledlow, carved on the chalk above its few houses. Whiteleaf deserves to be known for itself. The modernly made-up sound of its name—though more appropriately it was White Cliff two hundred years ago—suggests a recent growth, a suburb to Princes Risborough and probably built in the nineteen-twenties. In fact most of the cottages along its undulating, slightly twisting length of the Upper Icknield are two hundred years old, and they are set among trees in what must be the most leafy of village streets, and are pleasantly mixed—some local tile and brick, some thatched, some black-and-white. And if Whiteleaf possesses no parish church it has as its centre the Red Lion, adapted no doubt from a cottage-row. From its low-ceilinged bar there is a view between the chestnut trees that very few village pubs can equal. The patchwork of the clay vale stretches away as if without end.

A little beyond Whiteleaf, the Way is crossed by a lane coming

down Longdown Hill, near the foot of which is another hamlet, Cadsden, also with a noteworthy pub. At first glance it is a little surprising to find a pub there at all; Cadsden is so hidden along its bottom and so slight that even the one-inch O.S. map fails to name it: a mere group of no more than a farm, three cottages, and the Plough making up a brief street that ends at a gate (from which there is a footpath leading leisurely along a bottom into one of the quietest parts of the Chilterns). Why, everybody wonders, should a pub have been so sited, tucked away along a lane leading apparently to nowhere? The answer is to be found in the beech-woods that gather on every ridge. Originally only a farm cottage, the Plough acquired a bar for the bodgers and the tree-fellers of a hundred and more years ago. Today it draws its custom from farther afield, particularly from among those who like a choice of cheese with their drink; where else can you, in a country pub, be offered more than thirty varieties?

Great Kimble, so called to distinguish it from its even smaller neighbour Little Kimble, stands where the Upper Icknield, now A 4010, has to skirt round a wooded bluff. It is little more than a single street linking the two ways with its church at the top corner.

The church, very much restored about a hundred years ago when the tower was added, retains much of its thirteenth-century interior. It retains, too, a somewhat gloomy and forlorn atmosphere which may not seem inappropriate to those visitors who go there in search of its historical associations rather than its architectural qualities. There would seem to be few such visitors these days—though one can imagine that two or three generations ago democratically inclined fathers might have ushered their offspring into the place in order that they might stand where John Hampden had stood when he refused to pay his Ship Money. Of course until a decade or so ago some inkling of what Ship Money was and some idea of the part the Great Patriot had played in the early stages of Parliamentary democracy could have been expected, at least from children who as was said then 'had passed their scholarship'.

Nowadays, perhaps, we cannot expect such knowledge, at least not such an assumption of the heroism of the moment. We are too aware of the dictatorship which followed the Civil War and of what dictatorships can mean ... though to link Hampden's cousin, Cromwell, with our twentieth-century dictators is hardly fair either

to the man or the times. And, though heroic figures are no longer in vogue, John Hampden, and those he persuaded to join in his protest, were challenging the Establishment of the time, and an Establishment which, since judges were royally appointed to favour governmental wishes, could act as judge and prosecutor against its offenders—and in Hampden's case that could have meant loss of all property (and he was among the wealthier of local land-owners), and perhaps, if the seventeenth-century idea of treason could be proved, loss of life.

And if it had not been Hampden, someone else would have had to challenge the royal assumptions. The Ship Money demand was the last of a series of attempts by which the government headed by Charles I had tried, in defiance of accepted Parliamentary author-ity, to raise its income. Charles's advisers, more historically erudite than understanding, had dug back into medieval times for possible but antiquated sources of revenue: the ancient fee to be exempted from bearing arms was one—which, incidentally, Cromwell among others paid reluctantly; another was to demand, often from wealthy landowners, a fine for their ancestors' encroachments on what had centuries before been royal forests; and there was the formally dis-approved practice of 'monopolies'—which interfered with trade, raised prices, and generally offended the merchant class. All told, for most of what used to be called Charles's 'Eleven Years' Tyranny' the King and his advisers seemed almost to have intended to alien-ate those on whom kings normally relied for support.

Ship Money was merely one of such money-raising devices—the last, as it turned out, because after Rex *v*. Hampden had been decided there was little hope of collecting further taxes of dubious origin. Charles's advisers could make out something of a case for Ship Money; in medieval times kings had been empowered to de-mand the use of ships for coastal defence; under Elizabeth this practice had been replaced by a money tax on coastal towns; Charles could argue that to extend the tax over the hinterland was not unreasonable as defence of the coast was in effect defence of the whole country. But when to the argument was added the feudal notion that the King had an ancient right to demand money and supplies from all his subjects in time of national danger and that the King was 'sole judge of that danger', it was clearly time that the royal assertions were challenged.

Theoretically Hampden lost his case; but he lost in circum-stances which made it appear like a victory. Originally in July

1637 he had to face four judges, but when it began to look as if two might decide for Hampden, the proceedings were held up while a panel of twelve judges was chosen. But during that interval dissatisfaction with the royal government had erupted in His Majesty's northern kingdom; in August 1637 the Scots defied a royal attempt to foist the Anglican Prayer Book on them, armed themselves and threatened to invade England. It was in the turmoil that was leading to the fiasco of the Bishops' War that the Ship Money case drew to its close. Hampden was found guilty by the smallest margin possible: seven judges for the King, five for Hampden. Such uncertainty among royal nominees was assumed by His Majesty's opponents to demonstrate the illegality of Ship Money; and soon county sheriffs were reporting their inability to collect the tax ... while Hampden judged it advisable to evade further trouble by leaving the country for a while in the company of his cousin Oliver Cromwell. Their ship was, however, forbidden to sail and both returned home; but Charles for once did not press his legal claims.

In the sequel to these events, the incidents which led to the outbreak of the first Civil War in the autumn of 1642, Hampden played his part. Elected Member of Parliament for Wendover, he supported 'King Pym' in the series of attacks on the royal ministers and the royal power in the early sessions of the Long Parliament. He was one of the five Members whom Charles personally tried to arrest in the House—and ignominiously failed to catch. But whether, had the fortunes of war not taken him early from the scene, Hampden would have justified such assertions as Macaulay's 'the man who would have been, had he lived, the Washington of England' is debatable. Such a claim overlooks the difficulties Cromwell had to face; Hampden was never to know Cromwell's dilemma when Charles, after defeat, set about planning a second Civil War, and so destroyed any possibility of a compromise peace. Hampden, dying early, has gone down in history unsullied by association with the stigmas of Cromwell's dictatorship; he has become the martyred political hero, though these days that seems to count for less than it did. The reminder in Great Kimble church, a faded facsimile of the record of the Ship Money meeting showing the amounts demanded and the names of those who refused, is tucked away in a corner where only the curious will notice it. Today's visitors, it seems, are not expected to be interested.

Little Kimble church is, perhaps, more likely to appeal. The

Upper Icknield, as the road, has to take a sharp turn to avoid its churchyard, avenued with cypresses. A plain, simple thirteenth-century building, the church is more than locally famous for its wall-paintings; they were probably painted shortly after the church was finished and though time and damp have been unkind to them, it is possible to recognise eleven saints, including St Francis preaching to the birds (a rare subject in England), St George somewhat unexpectedly dismounted, and what is said to be the oldest St Christopher. There are traces of a 'Doom' on the west wall, and in the chancel is a set of medieval story-telling tiles.

Before the next village of Ellesborough with its church standing high on a spur is reached, the road passes the mound known as Cymbeline's Castle. Tradition has it as the site of a fortification raised by Cunobelin, a ruler of the late Iron Age Catuvellauni for some forty years between Caesar's invasion and the Roman Conquest and, a long time posthumously, the hero of Shakespeare's play. It is even asserted that Cunobelin's son was killed there in A.D. 43 resisting the invading Romans. Finds of Iron Age date tell that the neighbourhood was then settled; but Cymbeline's Castle, if it began as an Iron Age fort, has been adapted to a motte-and-bailey castle, probably in the decades following the Norman Conquest. In keeping with the local story, there is the site of a probable Iron Age village, later fortified by the Romans, in Brays Wood nearby (with what are believed to have been iron forges below), and the name 'Kimble' is said to derive from Cunobelin. But the Place-name Society ignores such a possibility. They offer 'cyne-bell', royal hill, which they could have attached to the local legend; but instead they suggest a nearby Chiltern crest.

The road abruptly twisting its way through Ellesborough village is skirting the park to Chequers, the Prime Minister's official country house. It is, however, hidden from the road and will have to be noted when sampling one of those lanes that lead into the hills.

By now Wendover is near, about the smallest town on the Icknield route and one of the most attractive—except to Robert Louis Stevenson, who found it 'a straggling purposeless sort of place'. It is in fact quite purposefully gathered about the crossroads where the Upper Icknield negotiates the gap made by the incipient Misbourne, and whichever way it is approached a mixture of eighteenth- and early nineteenth-century houses and shops and inns line the street. Probably the best are in Aylesbury Road which, as Pevsner

says, is 'flanked by nothing but attractive houses'; he could have added that they have been made even more attractive by the trees which the Wendoverians have kept along one of the wide verges. The Georgian look of the place suggests that it must have grown out of a village in the days of the stage-coaches. Before then it had achieved distinction by being sacked by the Royalists in 1643 and by becoming a parliamentary borough, including among its Members Hampden, of course, and later Burke, who is buried at Wendover, and Canning. It had back in the thirteenth century produced a distinguished historian at a time when historians were scarce—Roger of Wendover. Its history goes quite a lot further back, for Iron Age pottery has been found there and its name, though sounding very English in our ears, is Celtic: 'gwyn-dwfr', holy or fair water, and doubtless applied to a local spring, perhaps that which still feeds the stream that leads southwards to where, rather far from the homes of most of its parishioners, stands Wendover church. Like many of the churches hereabouts it has been rather obviously restored, at least externally. Inside it looks older, the chancel, the tower arch and one doorway suggesting the first half of the fourteenth century, and the nave a few decades later when the ravages of the Black Death were at last being overcome and builders were getting to work again and beginning to experiment with what was to become the peculiarly English medieval style Perpendicular Gothic. Could it be that Wendover church was one of those which was in the process of being built or rebuilt when the plague first struck with such devastation in the early summer of 1349?

Until recently Wendover had retained a further distinction: it had been divided—who knows how early in its history?—into two manors: 'Wendover Borough' and 'Wendover Forrens' (Foreign), and as recently as the early 1900s, when children from the outer 'foreign' areas were allowed to end their school day a quarter-hour earlier than those of the borough, it was the custom for the head-master to announce at a quarter to four: 'The foreigners may go home now.'

While the Upper Icknield for the six miles from Princes Risborough to the Wendover gap has been linking the villages, the Lower Icknield has been following its parallel way through fields with only an occasional hamlet on it; but from Wendover on to Akeman Street, it shifts unexpectedly northwards to take in Weston Turville and Aston Clinton. Whatever the reason for this behaviour

—it would seem of Roman origin—to follow the Lower Icknield through both villages would be to take William the Conqueror's route.

As has been mentioned, from Princes Risborough we have been following the footsteps of the Norman victors of Hastings. Ellesborough in particular suffered from the visit though it seems Wendover did not. William appears to have followed more the Lower Icknield, for Stoke Mandeville, a mile and a half to its north, and both Weston Turville and Aston Clinton were raided—collectively their post-1066 values had shrunk by about one-half. But it seems that somewhere among these villages a change of plan was formulated, for the Norman army's route takes three courses: one to turn northwards and bring trouble to the villages between Buckingham and Olney; another, possibly a minor force, left its mark through Linslade and Fenny Stratford; the third force kept on along Icknield until it had crossed Watling Street, after which it left a wider path of spoliation approaching Bedford from the south. This force was probably led by William in person for it appears to have visited—but not damaged—the manors of Leighton, Houghton Regis and Luton, once the property of King Edward the Confessor and now claimed by William as his successor. Icknield was to see the conquering army again only briefly when, having turned eastwards about Potton and apparently reformed into two columns, they crossed it near Baldock and Royston respectively, en route for Hertford, then already an important town and well placed as a base for an attack on London.

Both Weston Turville and Aston Clinton are largish villages spread around lanes that loop off the Lower Icknield, here green with roadside trees. Both are rather straggling places of mixed buildings with here and there among the brief terraces of Victorian labourers' cottages and the more recent additions, larger and more dignified red-brick farmhouses mainly of Stuart date. Weston Turville church, set among trees at the end of a lane, is worth finding. Nearby are the Georgian manor house and the earthen motte and double bailey of what was once an important castle. The church itself has architecturally something of almost every period from the thirteenth century onwards, and for the less architecturally inclined a discreetly placed showcase with such local items as fragments of medieval tiles, the churchwardens' records of rating assessments, and even their petty-cash books. And in the otherwise uncoloured glass of the east window there is a little

square from the fifteenth century, an expressive Virgin and Child like a gem.

At Aston Clinton this stretch of Icknield ends on the Akeman Street (A 41) leading to Tring, which Cobbett found in 1829 'a very pretty and respectable place'—but he had enjoyed a good dinner and was pleased with the reception of his stirring speech. Tring may still be respectable, but it is no longer 'very pretty'. It has suffered from two owners of the adjoining Tring Park— though later it benefited from one of them. Originally the town grew up along a stretch of Akeman Street, but towards the close of the seventeenth century Tring Park and its mansion were acquired by Sir William Gore, once Lord Mayor of London, who, disliking a main road through his estate, diverted it to its present somewhat uneven and meandering course. No doubt in time the new main street acquired a collection of Georgian houses and shops. And then in 1872 Lord Rothschild bought the Park. He rebuilt Gore's mansion—it had been designed by Sir Christopher Wren— and also reconstructed much of the town, demolishing the market house and the shops which stood about the church, and rebuilding many along the opposite side of the street in styles varying from what Pevsner calls 'architecturally deplorable' to the nondescript. Here and there a few pleasanter houses of eighteenth- or early nineteenth-century date survived, most of them about the fragment of Akeman Street, renamed Western Road, one of the best being the Britannia Inn, whose bold portico welcomes travellers coming from Aylesbury.

Somehow in all these changes Tring church has not suffered unduly. Though thoroughly battlemented, it looks less impressive externally than internally. It is now a substantial fifteenth-century church—the first so far on the Icknield route—not as striking as the fine fifteenth-century churches of East Anglia and the Cotswolds, but lofty and not without dignity.

The first item to catch the eye is the monument to Sir William and Lady Gore, which has stood opposite the main door since being moved from the chancel during the 1882 restoration. Probably the work of Nost, a pupil of Grinling Gibbons, it is unquestionably a good example of its period—early eighteenth century. Yet there is about it, as about many such monuments of that time, an uncertainty of pose—which suggests that one day a learned book should be written about such works, not so much about their craftsmanship as about the contemporary attitudes expressed in them.

Sir William and his Lady, half-reclining on the suitably concave sides of the plinth, look vaguely heavenwards, but their hands hint at a lingering awareness of earthly possessions: his left one fingers his insignia as Lord Mayor, hers touches a fold of her sumptuous dress. It is as if the sculptor, in keeping with the fashion of the time, had discarded the restful medieval pose with the figures prostrate and their hands uplifted in prayer, and the praying figures of late Tudor and Stuart times, but was unsure what other pose to try for. This perhaps tells us as much about the nobility of the early 1700s and later as do the inscriptions on their monuments.

Tring church has many details worth more than a glance, particularly overhead: the trusses of the ancient roof supported on little wooden angelic figures possibly representing the Apostles, and the collection of fourteen stone corbels, in the guise of the strange monsters that medieval man apparently thought should appear in a church. Some of these, such as the tusked antelope, the fox carrying the goose, the half-woman half-dragon, the 'wild man', and the monkey-headed friar, are to be found represented in many medieval churches but there is as yet no certainty as to their significance. Once Tring church had an even rarer sight: a set of medieval tiles which told a story, but these are now shared between the British and the Victoria and Albert Museums. The visitor to Tring has to be satisfied with photographs of them and explanatory notes.

Though the Rothschilds did not benefit Tring architecturally they gave the town its best-known attraction: its Natural History Museum, now part of the British Museum, and recently remodelled to show from almost every angle its immense collection of animals, birds and fish (not to mention a sizeable selection from its 2,000,000 insects). A visit makes one realise what an immense variety of animals are, or were, to be found. The modern ornithological department, open to the serious student, with over 1,000,000 perfectly preserved specimens stored in air-conditioned rooms, is probably the finest gathering in the world. Though only fortuitously in the Chiltern region, Tring Museum should not be missed.

Along Icknield from Risborough to Tring there are several lanes leading up through the beechwoods to the hamlets within the hills. It is still a region of sharp ridges and narrow bottoms intersected by lanes which at times seem determined to be as twisting and as hilly as they can.

The two most southerly routes have political flavours. A good starting-point for the first is the hill which climbs sharply from the south end of Whiteleaf village. At the hamlet of Redland End, among the trees immediately to the north a half-mile stretch of Grim's Dyke can be found, recognisable as unnatural but not impressive. Curiously after this half-mile it abruptly turns through a right-angle to cross Hampden Park and end at two barrows as yet unexcavated. The southward continuation of the Dyke behaves similarly: it turns an abrupt angle at Lacey Green to go a little east of south until it loses itself in the woods above Bradenham. But for the present we will take the lane through delightfully named Parslow's Hillock where between Pink Hill and Lily Bottom stands the Pink and Lily. It is a clumsy-chimneyed and very rural pub—a hatch still serves as the bar—and was even more rural when, in the months before the first World War, Rupert Brooke frequented it and wrote the lines which are to be found inside (but not in the *Collected Works*):

> Never there came to the Pink
> Two such men as we think
> Never there came to the Lily
> Two men quite so richly silly. ...

Brooke, it need hardly be added, also delighted in the country round about. 'Eddie [Marsh] and I had a perfectly glorious day yesterday,' he wrote from the Pink and Lily in June 1914 to Cathleen Nesbitt; 'we dissected and discussed and adjudged all the poets with infinite perspicacity and responsibility, and then we walked by those glorious woods to Wendover (you know the walk from Wendover, my dear) and drank much beer there and ate, and started back, and slept in the heather, and walked on through arcades of mysterious beechen gloom and picked flowers and told stories and got back to roast beef and more beer and poems. I wish you had been here.' Since that letter was written there have been many upheavals and many poets; but the poignancy that his early death brought to Rupert Brooke's poetry still lingers.

Two lanes go southwards, one dipping down Pink Hill through Loosley Row to meet the other again at Lacey Green. The upper one gives sudden views over the land spreading out beyond Princes Risborough. Both Lacey Green and Loosley Row are, or were, rather straggling places—though if it is assumed that Loosley acquired its name from its layout, the Place-name Society will put that right with

a derivation which reminds us that the Chiltern woodlands in medieval times served a purpose often overlooked: Loosley comes from 'hlose-leah', the pig-sty clearing.

From Lacey Green a lane to the east leads to Speen, a curiously up-and-down place. Here lies Eric Gill, sculptor and typographer extraordinary, and a rare person whose work although at the moment inclined to be overlooked will in time come to be revalued. The most noteworthy building in Speen is the Old Plow, an inn since 1610, approved by Pepys and much later kept by Ishbel, daughter of Ramsay MacDonald, the first Labour premier. The more southerly road leads eventually to Hughenden, site of a Roman settlement and now visited for its manor-house refashioned by Disraeli—it was his home for thirty years—and its church outside which he lies.

Perhaps more than any other building in the Chilterns Hughenden manor-house proclaims its originator. Appreciation must depend largely upon what one thinks of Disraeli. To those for whom he is a figure still to be revered, who admire the skill and tenacity which raised him from comparative obscurity and a racial handicap to the premiership, who delight in his verbal wit and dwell upon his vision of Empire, who recall the gratitude he earned from Queen Victoria to whom he was 'the kindest and most devoted as well as one of the wisest Ministers'—such admirers may find it easy to accept the architectural eccentricities of his home. But for those who are a little uneasy about this astutest of Victorian politicians who started as a Radical, joined the Tories only to split them before contriving to gain their leadership and then urged them as Conservatives into reforms that as Tories they would never have undertaken, and finally ushered in the New Imperialism—for those who so view him (and recall that before meeting the Queen he had said: 'everyone likes flattery; and when you come to royalty you should lay it on with a trowel'), Hughenden manor-house may seem uncomfortably what might be expected. The setting on the side of a tree-capped ridge seems very English; but the house ... One need not go all the way with Pevsner when he records in his *Buckinghamshire* how the 'unassuming' eighteenth-century house was 'ruthlessly dramatized' for Disraeli and that the details 'are excruciating, everything sharp, angular, aggressive. As much brickwork as possible set diagonally, the battlements stepped and with diagonally-placed pinnacles, the window-heads indescribable'; one does not have to be architecturally erudite to see that it is an odd showy

piece of work designed for an odd flamboyant character. Incredibly Disraeli believed that he had restored the place to what it had been two centuries earlier, a house in which 'cavaliers might roam and saunter with their ladye-loves'.

In the church nearby, remodelled at the same time as the house but not by the same architect, one can if cynically inclined find a parallel oddness in its most note-worthy features: a set of fake effigies by which an owner of the manor in Henry VIII's time had tried to acquire the appearance of a medieval ancestry. But it would be more fitting to note the memorial the Queen had put up near where Disraeli had sat each Sunday: 'Kings love him that speaketh right'; and outside the east end is the vault which the Queen asked to be reopened shortly after his funeral (which protocol forbade her to attend in person) in order that she might place a wreath of porcelain flowers on the coffin.

Or perhaps it would be kinder to Disraeli to leave Lacey Green by the lane that winds down through beechwoods to Bradenham, a village of warmly red cottages standing around a large, rectangular green with at the top, and backed by the rising woods, the late seventeenth-century manor-house in which 'Dizzy' lived during the years he was struggling to become a novelist or a poet and then a Member of Parliament. It is a gentler place in which to remember him, for the old house saw his happiest days and his early acquaintance with Mrs Wyndham Lewis who became his loved and loving 'Mary Ann' and, at his request, Viscountess Beaconsfield. In the screening woods must have begun his other great love—for trees. As he was to say later: 'A forest is like an ocean, monotonous only to the ignorant. It is a life of ceaseless variety.... I am not surprised that the ancients worshipped trees. Lakes and mountains, however glorious for a time, in time weary; sylvan scenery never palls.' When, overtired and ill and at the end of his momentous career, he left the capital for home it was, he said, to 'find repose in its woods'. Whatever may be thought of him as a politician or of the house at Hughenden he and his Mary Ann created, we who have known the Chiltern beechwoods can appreciate such feelings in the man.

Only a hundred yards from Bradenham is the Risborough–Wycombe road.

Another way through the hills, less hilly but no less political, starts from the hamlet of Butler's Cross a good half-mile on the Wendover side of Ellesborough. For the first mile and more it skirts

the park to Chequers. The house, standing on the floor of a wide bottom and set about with a variety of fine trees, many of which were planted long before it became the Prime Minister's country house, can be glimpsed from the road from time to time. It is red-brick, Elizabethan, and quietly dignified; later additions have been in keeping. It still retains its great hall and its long gallery now used as the library.

For those curious about the history of the house and how it came to be given to the nation as a country home for whichever Prime Minister happened to be in office, there are the opening chapters of D. H. Elleston's *Chequers and the Prime Ministers*. It seems that the odd name comes from the estate's owner at the time of Henry I, Elias de Scaccario, a Norman-French translation of whose surname is given as 'de Checkers', implying that he or one of his ancestors had been an official of the Exchequer. Thereafter, like so many ancient estates, it passed by marriage to other families—the Hawtreys, the Crokes, the Russells, the Astleys—and on the way was rebuilt about 1560/65; it became for two years the prison of Lady Jane Grey's sister (she had incurred Queen Elizabeth's wrath by marrying without royal permission and the room she occupied is still known as the 'Prison Room'); it was the home of Cromwell's daughter Frances and her descendants, and was eventually sold to Arthur Lee, a Conservative party figure in the decades before the first World War and later Viscount Lee of Fareham. It was he who in October 1917 gave the house, together with an endowment to maintain it, as a country home for future Prime Ministers. Elleston also tells of some of the objects of historical interest that are to be seen in the house and with which premiers have interested their guests: in particular the Cromwell relics, including the sword he is believed to have worn at the Battle of Marston Moor.

For those readers who like homely details about the famous occupants' lives at Chequers Mr Elleston gives occasional glimpses: Lloyd George often walked his dogs in the grounds, Baldwin being a countryman by birth was liked by the locals, Churchill entered in the visitors' book the birth of his grandson, the first time such a family occasion had occurred to a premier at Chequers. Most premiers have found the house a home as much as an official residence: Ramsay MacDonald: 'This place will find its way too deeply into my heart'; Stanley Baldwin: 'I owe more to Chequers than I can ever repay'; Neville Chamberlain: 'Chequers! ... It will be a hard wrench to part with that place where I have been so happy';

Winston Churchill: 'Our last weekend at Chequers was sad ... What distinguished guests it has sheltered, what momentous meetings it has witnessed, what fateful decisions have been taken under its roof.'

Perhaps not inappropriately the Chequers estate almost adjoins the Hampden land. The road leading southwards from Chequers follows a wide bottom between Great Hampden and Little Hampden.

There is no Great Hampden village. There are Hampden House, Hampden church and a scatter of houses known as Hampden Row about Hampden Common a half mile away. In one of them John Masefield wrote 'The Everlasting Mercy', acclaimed at the time of its publication but now less known than 'Sea Fever' and 'Cargoes'.

Hampden House is only occasionally opened to the public. At first glance—and little more than a glance is allowed to passers-by for it is screened with evergreen trees and so sited that little can be seen from the lanes round about—it appears mainly mid-eighteenth-century Gothick, excessively and decoratively battlemented. In it survive portions of earlier Hampden Houses: 'King John's tower' which, though King John is believed to have visited the Hampden of his day, is almost certainly a century later; the oak-panelled Hall, with its ancient roof, gallery and open fireplace, which welcomed Elizabeth I and James I; and the 'Patriot's Study' wherein John Hampden is said to have been served with the writ over his refusal to pay Ship Money, and some of its present furniture is said to have stood in it then. In the nearby church—mainly fifteenth century—there is a wall memorial to John Hampden put up in 1743, another to his first wife composed by Hampden, and brasses to two of his ancestors, but Hampden's own grave is unmarked. It is as if even in death he evades us. So often his great moment of defiance has been written about, and we know snippets of his political career, but the man evades us. He has attracted curiously few biographers. Was he, one wonders, a behind-the-scenes worker about whom we know little except when, for a few brief moments, he found himself in the political limelight?

By contrast with its greater namesake, Little Hampden is a more compact place, a string of farmhouses and cottages along a lane that leads only to its very wooded common. At one end is its diminutive church, mainly of the thirteenth century (of which date are the traces of wall paintings, too) though the massively timbered porch was added two hundred years later. At the other end of the village, almost surrounded by woods, is the Rising Sun,

VILLAGE GROUP

17. Thirteenth-century church, fifteenth-century lych-gate, eighteenth-century lock-up, at Anstey

18. Norman interior, Checkendon

CHILTERN CHURCHES

19. Fourteenth-century siting, Edlesborough

neat and unselfconscious—it has not been dolled up with a spurious antiquity to attract passing motorists because at its door the lane ends. Indeed the place looks as if it might have been created for families spending summer afternoons playing in the woods— though recently rather a lot of conifers have been planted and perhaps, in a few years' time, it may not look so inviting.

The road between the Hampdens leads on to Great Missenden, a long street of a place, pleasantly confined by its cottages and shops, with its church set well away from it, now across its bypass. When the church was built—in the fourteenth century though most of its windows must have been remodelled in the fifteenth—Great Missenden also had an abbey. It has one now on the same site, but it is for the most part a late eighteenth-century attempt at Gothic (for a London ironmonger who wished to appear a country gentleman) which has recently become a college.

Visually more attractive is Little Missenden, grouped round a minor crossroads (and also now bypassed). The Jacobean Manor House, a bold, brick house with a striking staircase projection, stands beside the churchyard; not far away is Missenden House, rather plain for its date (1729). The church is more than locally famous. Its walls are pre-Conquest; the nave arches were cut about 1120 in what had been the Anglo-Saxon walls, and the chancel arch was constructed in re-used Roman tiles. The chancel with its lancet windows was added or rebuilt in the thirteenth century, the north chapel early in the fourteenth, the tower and porch added a century later still, and the south aisle rebuilt in the 1700s. Its building life could be said to span the best part of a thousand years. Added to that, it possesses a collection of wall paintings ranging from about 1200 to the arms of Elizabeth I: St Christopher is there—twice—and a series of five scenes from the life of St Catherine; rather more fragmentary are a figure of Christ, a Nativity, and a 'Doom'.

Within a mile of each of the Missendens and on the north side of the Misbourne (which can hardly yet be regarded as a river) is a castle motte. The one a half-mile northeast of Little Missenden has a bailey, that southeast of Great may have had one (and it may have been a Norman reconstruction of an earlier 'fort'). Neither has as yet attracted expert investigation, and history, too, seems to be silent as to why two considerable works should have been raised within so short a distance.

A little way east of Little Missenden, the Wendover–Amersham

road, the end of this trip, is again reached. It offers a sight of Amersham's famous main street from the right approach. But the passer-by, having enjoyed its varied attractions—there is hardly a shop or house along it that does not tempt one to stop—negotiated its narrowing to pass the town hall, dated 1682, glimpsed the church tucked away nearby and been again delighted at the collection of buildings at the lower end—when he has had his fill of these the visitor should go on and not look back. Did the Amersham Victorians have to site the local gasworks so noticeably?

Leading from the section of Icknield between Wendover and Tring are a number of lanes which find their way, often a little reluctantly to judge by their sudden twists, to Chesham. The villages they link are, almost without exception, built along the ridges and so, besides often a house or two worth at least a glance, they offer good viewpoints of the neighbouring countryside, here rather less wooded (though tree-clumps are plentiful) and with more fields than formerly. At first sight there seems little about these villages that a passing glance will not satisfy; and yet when one looks a little more closely...

Take, for example, The Lee, a couple of miles southeast of Wendover: it appears just a random straggle of houses, some grouped around a little green, with as its church a suburban and uninspiring red-brick building, circa 1870. A closer look tells more. There is a rather disjointed length of Grim's Dyke curving southwards through the neighbourhood—southwards as if, unlike a normal defensive work, it is deliberately leaving open the valley in which the Missendens lie. And a mile to the east there is, half-hidden in Bray's Wood, another earthwork which may, or may not, be the site of a medieval homestead. And the church itself stands in a circular earthwork of age and purpose unknown. And by then the visitor will have noticed, behind the trees of Lee church, another much older building: a simple, thirteenth-century chapel, carefully restored to retain much of its original and very rural appearance and showing, very unexpectedly, Cromwell, Hampden and Miles Hobart in the glass of its east window. (They were made for Great Hampden church which declined them because Cromwell was included.) Perhaps because of its obscurity this little church has retained other oddments. Two of its lancet windows are elongated to allow the lower portion, originally unglazed but fitted with a wooden shutter, to act as what the ecclesiologist calls

'low side windows'. Such windows are believed to have once been common, but the theory which captured the fancy of Victorian church visitors—that they were opened to allow lepers standing safely outside to join in the services inside—has long been abandoned. Lepers would not have been allowed into the churchyard; the opening was more probably to allow the priest, in the days before the church could afford bells let alone a tower for them, to ring a handbell to tell the villagers that Mass time was near. The Lee's old church has also kept the staple holes to its ancient font though the staples have gone—a reminder of the medieval practice of locking the font cover so that the local witch could not use holy water for her unlawful and noisome concoctions. All told, The Lee has quite a lot to show.

So, too, have the villages of Cholesbury and St Leonards which spread themselves along a ridge about midway between Tring and Chesham. They are probably best reached from Icknield by a lane that climbs southwards from Tring. En route the most convincing stretch of Grim's Dyke may be viewed crossing the lane a mile and a half north of Cholesbury. On the western side it is traceable through High Scrubs Wood and across the fields nearby to The Lee; to the east it goes very clearly and determinedly for the best part of a mile and, after one of its puzzling turns, follows the ridge above the Bulbourne valley until nearing Berkhamsted it becomes fragmentary and peters out.

Even at the risk of emulating Alexander Pope's fool rather than his angel, some comments on this puzzling earthwork can no longer be evaded. The traveller is entitled to some guidance, and the experts—who tend to concentrate on more readily explicable forts and dwelling sites—can only suggest that it is possibly an intertribal boundary and offer either Iron Age or Anglo-Saxon workmanship. Such vagueness spreading over two thousand years will hardly satisfy those who like to know what they are looking at, while the imaginative may be put out to discover, after they have visualised woad-painted Britons manning the line, that they should have peopled it with Anglo-Saxon churls.

The name questions an Anglo-Saxon origin. Grim was an alternative name for their heathen god Woden. If the Dyke had been constructed on the orders of some Saxon leader it would, surely, have borne his name; indeed the length running from the Thames to Nuffield may have once been 'Ecgbeald's Ditch', referred to in a thirteenth-century document. But the other stretches of the Dyke

seem always to have been named after Grim. It is more than likely that the first Saxons to arrive hereabouts found the Dyke already there.

The course and the method of construction are against the Dyke's being a fortification or a boundary (which would, presumably, have had to be defended at times). The shape of both the main lengths—that between Hampden and Bradenham, and that to the south of Tring—form three sides of a rough square and keep to the higher ground, thus leaving the valley routes open; while it must be repeated that the ditch being on the inner side of the bank is wrongly placed to defend the area which the shape encloses. In fact when one walks along a length of the Dyke, and especially when one comes to one of the determinedly angular corners, it begins to look not so much intended to defend from outside as to contain what was inside. And the most likely occupants would have been cattle and sheep.

Such a suggestion, hinting that the mysterious Grim's Dyke may be no more than an elongated cattle fence, may disturb those who like to imagine earthworks as scenes of fierce encounters. It also implies that the area contained within each of the Dyke's roughly square courses was farmed on a large scale, was a kind of ranch supplying not mere household or tribal needs but an urban population elsewhere. This in turn suggests neither Iron Age nor early Anglo-Saxon origin, but Roman—for we know that many villas produced for the contemporary town markets. The Dyke would not, of course, have been the work of Roman engineers but could have been that of British slaves under Roman or Romanised overseers.

Such a suggestion also implies a centrally placed sizeable Roman settlement, the headquarters of the 'ranch'. For the more southerly stretch of the Dyke there is Hughenden where at least one Roman building has been found together with other finds hinting of more than a single, isolated building. The northerly area can, as yet, only be associated with the Iron Age fort at Cholesbury (which was, incidentally, occupied by Britons during Roman times); but it has, in a conveniently central position, the town of Chesham. The name is often assumed to be Anglo-Saxon—the 'ham' on the river Chess; but it was earlier 'Caester' or 'Caestel', a Roman settlement which gave its name to the river. Such a name implies that when the Saxons arrived more than a single Roman building was to be seen there....

It is time to resist the temptation of further guessing. One day perhaps an archaeologist's spade will tell us more. In the meantime along the lane leading southwards there are Cholesbury and St Leonards.

At first glance the only item to catch the eye in these villages is St Leonard's church. It prompts the adjective 'pretty'; there is a daintiness in its neat smallness, its white walls and its red roof topped with a little, spire-capped bell-turret. It was built or rebuilt about 1665, an unexpected date for few village churches were receiving much attention then. Its story is, indeed, far from pretty, as a glance at the list of incumbents inside hints. From its first vicar, installed in 1273, there is a sequence only until 1344; then comes a gap until 1632. It looks as though St Leonards suffered heavily when in 1349 the plague first struck; for more than two hundred years village life must have been at a low ebb and in 1522 the muster roll gives only eleven adult males.

A similar story seems to be told in Cholesbury's more restored church, though there the gap comes later—between 1415 and 1546. By 1563 only sixteen families are recorded. Like many another village on indifferent, upland soil it appears to have had a struggle to keep going.

Cholesbury's church has the distinction of standing within the prehistoric fort already mentioned, a point about which archaeologists have been showing curiosity recently. It suggests the possibility that sacred sites have survived far longer than was once assumed. We know that at the time of the Conversion of the Angles and Saxons, Pope Gregory the Great suggested to his missionaries that while pagan rites should obviously be discouraged, pagan shrines might be adapted to Christian worship 'in order that the people may the more familiarly resort to the places to which they have been accustomed'; place-names such as those containing 'harrow' from the Anglo-Saxon 'hearg', a shrine, imply that his advice was followed. But the siting of Cholesbury church hints at an even earlier possibility, that before Pope Gregory's time the pagan Saxons had already established shrines on the sites of Iron Age ones.

So much, and the mixture of houses from the late 1600s, a passer-by may glimpse hereabouts. For those who like to delve deeper there is much more, for St Leonards and Cholesbury are two of the four places covered in David and Joan Hay's *Hilltop Villages of the Chilterns*. Thanks to a lot of patient research, much

of the past of these villages can be rediscovered in this book. There are, for example, the little industries on which many a villager relied before the machine and mass-production closed them down: brick-making and pottery from the local clay, and straw-plaiting, which delighted Cobbett when he visited the Tring neighbourhood in 1829. The Hays also tell of the activities of the village constable called upon to arrest those guilty of 'prophane curseing and swearing'—not as one might expect in the Puritan decades but after the Restoration—and having to sort out the inevitable quarrels over the limited water-supply as when, in 1699, Mark Fenner was charged with 'turning the water out of the water-course which feedeth Thomas Kingham's mill'. Items quoted from the Poor Relief book tell of the villages' efforts to help their own poor: '1 shift for Ellen Cox and a pair of shoes.... Bread and Cheese and Beer for Forster's funeral.... Joe Cox be found work at the stone pit and be allowed 4d a load for breaking stone ... and he be paid partly in bread and partly in money, he being a drunken disorderly fellow'. For those who like to look deeper than the surviving visual impressions of the past the Hays' book is a find; and we must suspect that much of what they have discovered about a few of the Chiltern villages had parallels in many others. The 'good old days' were good only for some of the people some of the time.

SEVEN

Akeman Street to Watling Street

On the map of Roman Britain Akeman Street is one of the odder roads. It linked up with the famous Watling Street at Verulamium (St Albans), used the Tring gap to reach the clay plain, went heading with Roman directness through Aylesbury to Bicester and then bore away south of west for Cirencester (Corinium) where it met up with both the Fosse Way and a Roman road heading for Gloucester (Glevum) and South Wales. A road of some significance one would have thought, useful in the administration of Britannia, frequented by travelling merchants, and a military necessity if the inhabitants of Wales became restless. And yet not only have long stretches of it from Aylesbury onwards been reduced to mere dotted lines on the map—and marked slightingly 'course of'—but the crucial fifteen miles linking Verulamium and Tring have disappeared. Not until very recently have the indefatigable 'Viatores' traced its course—incidentally for much of the way it was a straight road alongside the present A 41, an irritatingly wavering and thoroughly un-Roman road if ever there was one—to the neighbourhood of Nash Mills near Hemel Hempstead where it took an abrupt left turn for Verulamium, apparently utilising an existing late Iron Age trackway.

Watling Street (A 5) is, by contrast, indisputably defined on the map and on the ground. Except for a few slight bends, and here and there a later deviation, it goes with the aggressive determination of a modern motorway. As it tackles the Chilterns from the northwest it does not, like Akeman Street, dither about and lose itself. It aims unerringly for the Dunstable gap and though thereafter it makes a slight concession to the fact that it is negotiating hilly country—it uses the slightly curving bottom in which Markyate stands—it straightens itself out again to head for Verulamium.

That Icknield between these two important roads was utilised by the Romans is certain; there is evidence of Roman occupation

in its neighbourhood including known buildings near Aston Clinton, Aldbury, Pitstone (two), and Totternhoe, and Dunstable, once Durocobrivae, was something of a town. But when the exact course of the Way or Ways is looked for there is little agreement between the experts. The O.S. map offers both an Upper and a Lower Icknield east of Akeman Street as far as Ivinghoe; the 'Viatores' found a minor Roman road taking a more southerly course than either, and climbing over Ivinghoe Hill. Such apparent disagreement may, however, not be contradictory. The Tring gap must into Roman times have been a somewhat marshy area; no doubt before then its users had varied their route according to the weather conditions and how much wading they were prepared to do. Not unnaturally these varying routes would have tended to converge on Ivinghoe below its boldly thrusting Beacon Hill. Thereafter according to the map Icknield becomes singular; but, as has been mentioned earlier, there is from Ivinghoe village a sequence of track and footpath continuing the Lower Icknield's line which may have been an ancient way. On the map and on the ground it behaves very like the more southerly stretches of the Lower Icknield—a quiet, gentle, easy-going way through fields—and significantly it passes very close to the mound on which Edlesborough church stands and climbs over the spur above Totternhoe to go near to 'Maiden Bower', an Iron Age fort which was raised above a Neolithic site.

All of which may perplex those impelled by historical accuracy, but may suggest to the less committed traveller a selection of routes from which to choose a way to his liking. From Tring he can by taking the allegedly Lower Icknield make the acquaintance of Drayton Beauchamp—its church set apart from the village under a rising wood has two fine fourteenth-century brasses and a rare 'Creed' window among its attractions—and Marsworth, the church of which has an unusual brass depicting a death-bed scene and may intrigue the architecturally knowledgeable for it is a remodelling of a fourteenth-century church by a late Victorian vicar and his wife (who actually undertook some of the work). Most visitors to Marsworth are more likely to be attracted to the quiet reaches of the Grand Union canal below the village and to the Red Lion of welcoming red-brick, old-village-inn appearance. Or if on foot the traveller can follow the canal towpath with, perhaps, a detour to take in one or other of Tring's reservoirs, now nature reserves. Either way the passer-by will notice en route that eighteenth-century wonder, the Grand Junction canal (now named the Grand

Union), for fifty years an arterial route for Britain's trade which made busy and alive the hamlets of Tring Wharf and Bulbourne. He should not overlook a nineteenth-century wonder, the cutting by which the railway makes its way through the lower slopes east of the gap. Constructed by 'Rocket' Stephenson's son, it was in its day the most impressive cutting that the railways could boast; when under construction it is said to have drawn crowds of sightseers.

Or by a slight detour from the most southerly of the suggested Icknields, and possibly itself yet another ancient route across the gap, there is the lane to Aldbury.

Of all the Chiltern villages Aldbury is the most widely known from its photographs. It has just about everything a village should have: an ancient church, a variety of old brick and brick-and-timber cottages set about a village green complete with stocks, whipping-post and a pond in which to reflect its attractions, and for a backdrop beechwoods climbing the sharp slope up to the hill-top common it shares with Pitstone and Great Berkhamsted. There can be few more photogenic villages in the country; and if that hints of superficiality, perhaps that is not wholly inappropriate. Attractive as Aldbury is, it shows itself almost too readily. Closer study reveals little more. The newer houses, built no doubt for those non-Aldburians who have found the place an escape from a suburb, are mostly discreetly screened by the village-green-surrounding older houses; the church, though of thirteenth-century origin and mainly of fourteenth-century workmanship, is almost too well cared for and its most noteworthy feature, a fifteenth-century chapel complete with contemporary screen, is not truly in situ but was brought from Ashridge, as was also the fine brass of 1546. Perhaps the most unusual item in the village—and one which hasty passers-by can overlook and many of those who wander around camera in hand scarcely glance at—is the tall-chimneyed village bakehouse with its large porch which served as the well-house. It is, like the almshouses behind it, of early Victorian date, but even so is a rare reminder of the days before bakers' roundsmen (let alone sliced and packaged bread), when the risk of fire if cottagers undertook their own baking prompted landowners to build a communal bakehouse. Once village bakehouses must have been quite common—in the Middle Ages villagers were sometimes required to use them and to pay the unavoidable due—but few are now to be found.

For the walker the obvious way from Aldbury to Ivinghoe is up through the woods and along the crest to the Beacon standing out finely and giving great views over the clay vale and along the sweeping escarpment. On the way he will pass the Monument, a Doric column to the third Duke of Bridgewater, the 'father of inland navigation', though for a life-long woman-hater—he would scarcely allow a woman servant in his presence—'father' seems rather too domestic a title. And his monument here on the Chiltern crest is, truly, a little out of place for though he was buried in his family home at Ashridge, a couple of miles away (and rebuilt since his day), he lived for most of his life on his estate at Worsley, Lancashire. There started his first effort at canal-building to carry, more easily and more cheaply, coal from his mines at Worsley to Manchester. His partner in the enterprise and the engineering genius was that strange, illiterate former millwright, James Brindley. How they together solved the problem of carrying their canal over the River Irwell by an aqueduct—an idea that was ridiculed as impossible before it was done—has often been told. The impressive result became one of the great sights of the time, even drawing viewers from abroad, and prompting such accounts as that of a visitor in 1764: 'I have lately been viewing the artificial wonders of London, and the natural wonders of the Peaks; but none of them gave me so much pleasure as the Duke of Bridgewater's navigation.... At Barton Bridge he has erected a navigable canal in the air.... Whilst I was surveying it with a mixture of wonder and delight, four barges passed me in the space of three minutes, two of them being chained together, and dragged by two horses who went on the terras [tow-path] of the canal whereon, I must own, I durst hardly venture to walk, as I almost trembled to behold the large river Irwell underneath me, across which this navigation is carried by a bridge ...'

Similar eulogies added to the Duke's and Brindley's fame and the idea of a wider use of canals caught on. Certainly their joint achievement, a canal system linking the major navigable rivers of England, owed more to their works than to their personalities. The Duke appears always to have been a remote figure, indifferent to what people thought of him and so disliking 'ornament' that on one occasion he uprooted the flowers planted at Worsley ... though the workers on his estates and in his mines were to say of him that he was a just master, albeit a stern one. Almost his only topic of conversation was canals. One gets the impression that he was at

heart a lonely, uncomfortable man, which is perhaps why he could team up with the uneducated Brindley, who it is said was incapable of the necessary draughtsmanship and—one can still wonder at the rare ability—retained in his head the calculations and planning needed in the construction of their many joint 'navigations', though when a particularly troublesome problem arose he needed to go to bed to think it out. A strange partnership; one day perhaps some psychologist will explain it.

By the time the Grand Junction canal, making its way through the valley below the Duke's monument, was being constructed— in 1792—the Bridgewater–Brindley dream of a national canal system had become a reality. They had constructed over 350 miles of canals and more were being planned. Before the first barges could negotiate the locks that climb from the Aylesbury plain to the Tring gap, both Brindley and the Duke were dead; but they had produced an efficient (if rather slow to our thinking) method of goods transport without which the Industrial Revolution would probably have staggered to a halt on the contemporary, inadequate and hazardous roads. On the eve of the next revolution in transport, the railway, Britain had over 4000 miles of canals—which, had they all survived in usable condition, would have provided a wider range for those who enjoy the canals' leisurely way of holiday-travelling. Perhaps the passer-by should give a grateful glance towards the Duke's monument for that unintended outcome of his and Brindley's efforts—though they would hardly have been gratified that their joint achievement should end as a minor if pleasurable holiday route.

For the motorist the lane from Aldbury to Ivinghoe passes, if not another monument, a house that was once the home of one nearly as well known as the Duke. The house, 'Stocks', stands back from the road, little more to be seen than its formerly famous occupant is to be remembered. Does anyone nowadays read Mrs Humphry Ward's *Robert Elsmere* which in the 1880s we are told 'swept into every drawing-room in England', and even prompted a detailed study by Mr Gladstone? Or her later *The Case of Richard Meynell*? They were certainly far from the light romances of the day which we might expect to have enjoyed only transient popularity; they were serious works, expressing their writer's striving for a return to the social content in Christianity. In keeping with her convictions, Mrs Humphry Ward founded a settlement to practise her ideas among the poor of London, pioneered special

education for the physically handicapped and, though she could not bring herself to venture into politics, promoted through her Women's Anti-Suffrage League the idea of women, though still to be voteless, bringing their views to the attention of their male representatives. A restless, energetic, deeply religious woman, she seemed in her lifetime to have achieved lasting fame; but the immense appeal of her novels, and the interest in her social work, arose more because she expressed the view of the socially advanced of her time. Since then her assumptions of charity, very Victorian in our eyes, have become suspect, and her didactic style, as well as her social attitude, find in us far less response than they did in the 1890s. She was of her time and that time has passed. She lies now in Aldbury church remembered perhaps more as aunt to Julian and Aldous Huxley (who often visited Stocks) than for herself.

Along the lane from Aldbury to Ivinghoe the appearance of the Chiltern crest changes. The hills above Aldbury are still rich with beechwoods; indeed the two square miles of woodland that stretch from Aldbury Common almost to Ashridge and reach from above Berkhamsted nearly to the eastern slope of Ivinghoe Beacon are as fine as any to be found in the length of the Chilterns (and are protected by the National Trust); but they are also the last of the ridge-top woods. Even before the bold rise of Ivinghoe Beacon is reached the hills have acquired a barer, firmer look. Only a few scant thorn-bushes break the rise of the escarpment; and the outline of the hills, boldly rounded, stands up against the sky without the softening of woodlands. And so it is on to Dunstable and beyond—at least when viewed from Icknield. The walker taking the crest route—and if he wishes for a footpath way, he will need a map to guide him across the hollow in which the hamlet of Dagnall lies and up on to the fine sweep of the Dunstable Downs—will see that all is not so treeless as appears from below the escarpment. The gentler slopes to the southeast have patches of woodland, some of them quite large, among their fields. But the character of the landscape is changing; the bottoms are becoming less sharply defined, the ridges tend to be broader, and the lanes linking the villages, though still demanding a watchful eye from the motorist, are less abrupt in their hills. There is a hint of the smoother, sweeping country with which the Chilterns end.

According to the geologists the ice sheet of the third Ice Age did not reach so far westwards as Ivinghoe, and certainly the

sharp rise of the escarpment would confirm them; yet the barer look of the crest, suggesting that the clay-with-flints cover of so many of the Chiltern ridges is hereabouts very thin, makes one wonder what other agency has been at work in geological times. Or can it be that the apparent bareness is not wholly natural in origin? It may have been that the hills beyond Ivinghoe Beacon were early cleared of their thin natural covering by the local sheep and goats—that the region was comparatively intensively settled is implied by the Iron Age 'forts' above Ivinghoe and Totternhoe— and perhaps continuity of grazing left no opportunity for the crest to regain what thicker natural growth it might support. Whatever the reason, the Chilterns are becoming less wooded, but scarcely less dramatic in their shaping.

For the traveller along Icknield there are other visual changes in the villages that lie a little to the north of his route. Ivinghoe village possesses some pleasant houses, perhaps the best of them the eighteenth-century house that serves now as a Youth Hostel; but soon the Way leads into Bedfordshire where brick is the local building material, and not the gently red brick of further south but for at least the last century and a half a harder, greyer or chillier brick. Here and there earlier survivals possess timber frames; but most of the cottage-rows have a work-a-day appearance. Their character is less appealing to those who delight only in 'pretty villages'; they attract few photographers.

By way of compensation the village churches along this stretch of Icknield are remarkably good. They were built or rebuilt early in the thirteenth century, probably under John de Cella, the 'building abbot' of Dunstable, who was born at nearby Studham. It was a time of growing prosperity when many a village sprouted hamlets into previously uncultivated land and so caused what historians refer to as the 'colonisation of the wastes'.

Pitstone's is the first of these churches and the most forlorn, being nowadays overshadowed by a large cement works which often spreads a pale dust over the place; but it is worth borrowing the key to look inside the church with its rich twelfth-century font and its elaborate Jacobean pulpit. Ivinghoe is the largest of the group; its impressive proportions deserve Pevsner's adjective 'noble', while the details of gargoyles and ornament are remarkably good. Edlesborough, on so abrupt and isolated a hill that it looks artificial, is the most strikingly situated, and has inside much good woodwork including an intricately carved pulpit complete with a rare

contemporary canopy, a fine screen, and six misereres with their strange underseat carvings—the most nearly human is the mermaid mothering a diminutive beast—and their arm-rests adorned with beings varying from angels to harpies. (This church also has the only surviving 'rose brass', small, simple, and dated 1412—and reminding that the rose was a familiar badge long before Henry Tudor borrowed it.) The last of the series is Eaton Bray, internally the most enchanting.

These four churches are all in the style known as Early English —a misnomer for it came from the Continent—the first pointed-arched, slim-columned, lancet-windowed style of which Salisbury Cathedral, slimly beautiful externally, austere within, is one of the purest examples. It is the style we saw beginning at humble Radnage; in Ivinghoe and Eaton Bray it has become freed from the earlier crudeness—a leftover from the Norman way of building —and is acquiring a richness that hints of the so-called Decorated style to follow. The capitals of the slimmer columns have now acquired the beginnings of leaf-patterned adornment, the unfolding bud-shape known somewhat unsympathetically as 'stiff-leaved'; the lancet windows, now grouped in threes or fives under a single arch are, as in Edlesborough's fine east window, being enriched with tracery that during the next half-century is to grow into some of the most exquisite stone carving that is to be seen, such as the east window of Carlisle Cathedral or the west window of York. These village churches cannot, of course, vie with such splendours, but they have a lightness and an appeal which makes a glance into any one of them an experience. They are from a time when religious enthusiasm was growing. Life was still harsh and often brief but it held hope and faith. Wars, famines and pestilences were familiar occurrences but conviction had not yet suffered the widespread shock of the Black Death and the questioning that followed it.

Only a mile from Eaton Bray's church is Totternhoe's and there can be seen in stone the change that took place. Built a full century after the others, Totternhoe church reflects a different feeling, a changed outlook. Its style is what is now known as Perpendicular Gothic; the name, when applied to the window tracery, is apposite. Gone is the spontaneity of the Decorated windows; gone, too, are the leaf-sprouting, growth-suggesting capitals of the columns and the freer feeling expressed in stone. Though the windows are wider, the columns slimmer and the whole building lighter and more

airy, there is about the style a rigidity and a mechanicalness—no wonder we can read of stone-masons no longer working for individual churches but producing something near standardised units. Not that these fifteenth-century churches are devoid of interest; indeed many have an unsurpassed dignity (and Totternhoe's has had since 1971 the added distinction of an east window designed by John Piper). And yet often there is a lack of individuality. They hint that the earlier inspiration is flagging, though their rich details may tell that materially the country has recovered from the calamities of the last half of the fourteenth century. They are of the age when much, but not all, of England thrived on the wool trade, even while its nominal rulers were committing political suicide in the Wars of the Roses. It was the age that followed not only the Black Death but also Wycliffe and his Lollards who in the opening decades of the fifteenth century won sympathisers among the members of the House of Commons and threatened to disturb the ancient power of the Church. In the reaction, questioning was discouraged, obedience was demanded and at times cruelly enforced. It was an uneasy time when safety lay in accepting and in clinging to the known. Below the surface had begun the ferment that, finding an excuse in Henry VIII's matrimonial activities, was to produce the Reformation. Something of this is reflected in the sameness of the churches; only the carvers in stone and wood indulged their fancies in their curious figures and faces.

Both Eaton Bray and Totternhoe have more to show the passer-by. Eaton Bray once had a castle, built in King John's time without royal permission by William de Cantilupe; he was one of the barons who opposed the King and so was instrumental in bringing about Magna Carta—though whether his opposition grew from principle or merely from a reluctance to contribute to John's demands for funds to pay for the unsuccessful French war, history does not tell. The moats and earthworks of Cantilupe's castle—more probably a well-defended manor-house—can still be seen at the west end of the village.

Totternhoe is noteworthy for its curious name and the ancient quarries on the far side of the bold, elongated spur above the village. The way this spur juts out prompted early recognition of its strategic possibilities. Neolithic people constructed an enclosure on it—perhaps a village-protecting rampart, perhaps a cattle pound—which the Iron-Agers adapted into what is now known as 'Maiden Bower'. The Normans erected a motte-and-bailey castle at the

western end so that it was additionally defended by the steep rise from the plain. Between those times the Saxons also used the place and gave it its name: the 'hoe' from 'hoh', a hill-spur, is only to be expected hereabouts, but 'tote-aern', the look-out house, takes us back to the time of the Danish invasions, if not earlier. The *Anglo-Saxon Chronicle* tells that in 876 the Danes under Guthrum rode from their camp at Cambridge to Wareham in Dorset (where King Alfred besieged them and compelled them to leave without payment); they would almost certainly have travelled via Icknield. So it would have been about that time, perhaps as part of Alfred's defence system, that the look-out house that gives Totternhoe its name would have come into use. Totternhoe's is the best-known of these Chiltern look-out points; in his *Archaeology of South-east England*, Gordon J. Copley has given many more, though most survive in minor place-names such as Ward's Hurst on Ivinghoe hill ('ward' derives from the Saxon for 'guard') and Wayting Hill (a 'wait' was originally a watchman) a little beyond where Icknield, north of Luton, swings eastwards. (The practice of using the crest for look-out points was revived in 1796 when Napoleon threatened invasion. One of a series of 'signalling towers' was erected between Dunstable and Kensworth, so sited as to receive and pass on information about hostile fleet movements observed from Yarmouth. It was dismantled in 1814.)

Totternhoe stone, though quarried at least from early medieval times, had to wait until the mid-eighteenth century before the workings were visited by one capable of leaving a record of how the stone was mined. Kalm, a Swedish visitor who travelled hereabouts, tells how the stone was reached by way of a long passage which not only ran with water during the winter but also 'after six to seven fathoms into the mine' was 'coal-black darkness as of night'. Other passages led from the original one, making 'the worst labyrinth and maze there could possibly be'. Along these passages the workers hacked out the stone with picks or hammered iron wedges into the rock 'by which they spring it loose'. The stone was then loaded on to a low wooden truck running on wooden rollers and dragged to the entrance before being wound by the windlass to the nearby space where the stone was roughly squared. The resulting clunch was, however, not an ideal building stone; it could be easily carved but did not weather well. It is often to be seen, usually having received some resurfacing, forming the corners or framing the door and window openings in many a Chiltern

20. *Fifteenth-century town opulence, Hitchin*

CHILTERN CHURCHES

21. *Thirteenth-century village simplicity, Radnage*

22. *Market Hall,*
Watlington

PLACES OF WORK

23. *Post Office,*
Westmill

church though for the actual walls flint was more often used.

Totternhoe is now a long, rather straggling village under the southwestern slope of its hill. At one end, below the Norman castle motte, is the remains of a homestead moat; at the other opposite the church a Roman villa once stood. The place has had a long life, and recently towards Dunstable closes of new houses have enlarged it.

One would expect Dunstable, on the crossing of Icknield and Watling Street, to be a venerable place with traces of its ancient origin; but in spite of its obvious position it has not enjoyed continuity. New Stone-agers, Bronze-agers and Iron-agers knew the neighbourhood and have left their various earthworks on the hills around, notably 'Maiden Bower' already mentioned and the 'Five Knolls', a collection of round barrows on Dunstable Downs, Though classified as a Roman 'posting station', little is known about it but its name of Durocobrivae. Though Watling Street survived through the once 'Dark Ages', few Angles or Saxons appear to have settled there though they used a Bronze Age barrow on the Downs for their dead, more than a hundred of them, probably the casualties from an unrecorded battle. And even Henry I's refounding of the town seems not to have ensured prosperity. The royal residence of Kingsbury at times attracted custom to local traders and no doubt Dunstable's innkeepers benefited from the tournaments held under Henry III (who disapproved of them and preferred to visit Dunstable Priory) and Edward I and Edward III. But tournaments with their 'counterfeited feats of warre' though splendid affairs were rather occasional; between them the people of Dunstable had to rely on passers-by.

Perhaps the clue to Dunstable's shortcomings is to be found in its priory of Augustinian canons founded by Henry I in 1131. A town dominated by a monastery tended to be retarded in its growth; whereas a lay or a royal landlord would, for a payment and a share in the profits, allow a town to become a borough and so, under the control of its leading merchants, develop its business, monastic landlords were often too determined to maintain their rights over their possessions to grant borough status. Such a situation not infrequently gave rise to conflict; the detailed history of many a town controlled by a monastery is punctuated by disorders and revolts. When briefly in the summer of 1381 it seemed that the 'commons' might achieve some freedom from the ancient and irksome restrictions—and townspeople as well as serfs joined in

the Peasants' Revolt—Dunstable was the only Chiltern town which saw serious trouble. Its story is very similar to that of St Albans whose townspeople similarly suffered from the power of its Abbey. Hearing of the successes of the followers of John Ball and Wat Tyler—the rebels had been allowed within the walls of London and had even occupied the Tower—and believing in the freedom-granting charters the young Richard II was persuaded to issue to encourage the rebels to disperse, the leading townsmen of Dunstable demanded of the prior, Thomas Marshall, a similar charter freeing them from the limitations imposed by the priory and allowing borough status. Like the abbot of St Albans, to whom a similar demand had been made, the prior gave way, and the charter was duly prepared; but when the news came of Tyler's death and the sudden collapse of the revolt, the Dunstable charter like the St Albans one was at once withdrawn ... though Dunstable was not to suffer the harsh punishment that St Albans knew. Prior Marshall appears to have been a more humane man than the Abbot de la Mare for, instead of demanding the full penalty, he persuaded the King's judges to treat the local rebels leniently.

Dunstable Priory is one of the few monasteries for which details of its dissolution have been published, telling of the pensions paid to its religious and giving some clues as to what became of them. The last Prior, Gervase Markham, who surrendered the house on 31 December 1539, received a pension of £60 a year until he died in 1561. The sub-prior's pension was £9, those for the ten canons varied from £8 to £2, and all but one received the living of a parish church. With this addition the canons' incomes ranged from £11 to £46 a year—though Canons Augustine Curtis, Robert Somer and John Nyxe, having married, were deprived of their livings when Mary Tudor came to the throne. These figures look ridiculously meagre to us—until we recall that in Henry VIII's time a labourer earned from £6 to £8 a year and a skilled craftsman no more than £12.

The Dissolution offered Dunstable only a brief prospect of more stable prosperity. The idea of making the priory one of Henry VIII's new cathedrals was soon abandoned. It was not until the middle of the eighteenth century when roads began to be improved and transporting became easier that Dunstable started to grow beyond its original 450 acres—and by then it had at last acquired an industry: straw-plaiting for the making of straw hats. Its good communications enabled it to share the industry with its

larger neighbour: Luton produced mainly for the mass market, Dunstable went in for higher quality. By the time straw hats were going out of favour other, newer industries were being established at Dunstable, attracted by the nearness of the London market and the new accessibility offered by the railways.

From all its chequered history Dunstable has retained little: a few eighteenth-century houses and a fragment of its priory, the first conventual building since we left Goring. This remnant seems almost out of place in modern Dunstable though there have been attempts—a little too obvious ones to the west front—to make the place attractive. Internally it has the solemnity of a Norman cathedral with its massive columns supporting round arches—here the columns are no longer stolid units but are shaped as if hinting at the groupings that the Early English style was soon to bring. But the place is essentially pathetic, a fragment of what once was. The present chancel occupies the centre of the original monastic church; the great central tower, the transepts, and the long choir have all vanished (as have also the monastic buildings). And the nave's former loftiness has been destroyed with the removal of its clerestory. These losses may have been historically inevitable; the townspeople, who had long used the nave as their parish church, would have found it difficult to have kept the whole building in repair. But for today's visitor the place seems out of proportion, its massiveness almost clumsy, and forlorn. Nor can it show much of interest in the way of monuments though it has recovered the remarkable Fayrey Pall. Eight feet long and made of Florentine velvet on cloth of gold, this attraction for visitors was presented by Henry and Agnes Fayrey about 1520 to the Fraternity of Dunstable burgesses at whose burials it was used as a coffin cover. It was confiscated at the Dissolution, recovered by the churchwardens in 1812 (and used for funerals at sixpence a time), lost again until 1883 when it was found among the possessions of a deceased incumbent, and finally restored to the church in 1891. Perhaps one day the brass to its original donors will also be sent back to Dunstable; it is now in the Victoria and Albert Museum.

Before progressing along the next stretch of Icknield let us glance at a few of the places within the hills.

First there are the Gaddesdens, approachable along the lane that climbs around Ivinghoe Beacon and then makes its way through the woods that skirt Berkhamsted Common. It is a ridge-

top way for the most part, giving green glances into the bottoms on either side. Little Gaddesden is reached first, a long village with fine trees on the lane-side green. An outstanding timber-framed house is allegedly the home of John of Gaddesden, physician to Edward III, but it appears about a century after his time. Further along is the manor-house of 1576, occasionally open to the public and of special interest for its collection of early keyboard instruments; nearby is an impressive octagonal dovecote. Great Gaddesden, which looks the smaller, is more compact; it is an up-and-down mile to the northeast of Nettleden, the gay hamlet at which the ridge ends.

Each Gaddesden has a church that is interesting, if the visitor does not mind a somewhat sobering subject, for its monuments. Those at Little Gaddesden—the church is, by the way, set apart from the village at the end of a lane—are mainly to the Egerton Earls and Countesses of Bridgewater; those at Great Gaddesden— the church is tucked away behind a farmyard—are to the Halsey family. And collectively they cover the period from 1611 to 1829, those awkward centuries that we noticed first in Tring church. The restful and recumbent pose used throughout the Middle Ages and into Tudor times had been discarded and sculptors seemed to be seeking for some other way of recording in stone not only the virtues but also an impression of the dead. The earliest one (1611) —over the door at Little Gaddesden—shows the fashion of late Elizabethan and Jacobean times: a kneeling figure, here in vivid red, with the inscription tucked underneath. But by the close of the seventeenth century such figures had been abandoned at least in this neighbourhood, and for a time no representation appears. The monuments, though still impressive in size, are limited to inscriptions, sometimes on stone 'drapery' held up by cherubs, putti, or other diminutive infants who may look tearful or pleased. (Here and there a skull appears in their company.) As if such memorials were held to lack individuality, profiles and, later, busts are introduced within canopied frames; indeed four of the Halseys of Great Gaddesden, ranging from 1719 to 1739, look so similar that one feels tempted to think of mass production. Within another century, however, such representations are going out and vaguely allegorical figures appear: a child angel holding a book on which a text appears (1782 at Great Gaddesden), a group of idealised farming folk (1823 at Little Gaddesden). Somewhere in all this display should be discernible more than what the monuments

show: something of how the dead, or their sorrowing relations, thought about such an unavoidable subject. Perhaps somebody will one day write a book interpreting such monuments more fully— and perhaps let us know how so many of the ladies came to be depicted in what Jane Austen called the 'first bloom' even though they often lived to a good age. In the absence of photography and the unlikelihood of portraits showing conveniently posed profiles, could these eighteenth-century people have followed the medieval custom and been sculptured from life in readiness? Should we try to imagine, say, a young husband addressing his new wife: 'My dear, how lovely you look this morning! I must get on to Nollekens —the monument sculptor, you know—so that he can capture your beauty so that when the time comes...'? It would be interesting to know.

From Great Gaddesden it is only a short way to the much photographed hamlet of Water End on the River Gade and from there to Hemel Hempstead, approaching from the right direction: first the Norman church and the High Street with its early eighteenth-century shops and houses, then on to the New Town already looking a little dated but no less interesting for that, and ending at the more recent tower blocks. Or before leaving the Gaddesdens there is Ashridge House, now the Bonar Law College, once the home of the Earls and Dukes of Bridgewater. Like so many great houses it stands on the site of an earlier Tudor one which in turn replaced a monastery dissolved at the Reformation. The present Ashridge House dates only from 1814/20, and is one of the most striking examples of what is known as the 'Gothic Revival'. Designed by James Wyatt and completed by his son, Sir Jeffry Wyatville—a knighthood in those days apparently required an addition to the family name—Ashridge is a triumph ... at least to those who accept the idea of building a mansion in an adaptation of a style that had been evolved for ecclesiastical buildings and the great halls of manor-houses. To others it may appear rather as an elaborate conceit in stone. But even they can delight in Ashridge's setting. It is almost surrounded by some of the finest of beechwoods, and an adjacent tongue of more open and wilder land forms Berkhamsted's common across which a lane reaches that town by way of the site of its castle.

Once the home of kings and princes, Berkhamsted castle is now little more than the mound of its motte and the hollows of its double moat, with a few fragments of wall. Great Berkhamsted

itself has more to show: a church originally early thirteenth century with several brasses, a much-restored sixteenth-century Court House, a row of seventeenth-century almshouses and several eighteenth- and early nineteenth-century houses, big and small, many of the best of them in side streets. Only belatedly, however, does Berkhamsted appear to have tried to live up to Southey's claim that it would 'be more known in after ages as the birthplace of William Cowper than for its connection with so many historical personages who figured in the tragedies of old'. The rectory in which Cowper, one of the most lovable and tragic of poets, was born has been rebuilt; not until a century after his death was the memorial window to him inserted in the church's Lady chapel, not far from where his mother lies. Otherwise there is nothing at Berkhamsted to remember him by; except, perhaps, in the country round about. His feelings for that countryside permeate his poetry. As he wrote to a friend in 1759 when, worn down by the sufferings that had started in his unhappy schooldays and had been added to by disappointment in love and the death of his father which, he knew, would cause him to leave Berkhamsted for ever: 'There was neither tree, nor gate, nor stile in all that country to which I did not feel a relation.' The 'stricken deer that left the herd long since', as he described himself and his inability to find restful association with his fellows, was sinking into the mental illness that was to dog him for the rest of his life:

> See the shadows of evening, how far they extend,
> And a long night is coming, that never may end.

Berkhamsted can claim three other literary associations: Graham Greene was educated at Berkhamsted school where his father was headmaster, W. W. Jacobs whose multitude of short stories delighted our fathers and grandfathers lived in the town, and James Barrie often visited Berkhamsted to which his friends, the Llewellyn Davises—one of whose sons was the original of Peter Pan—had moved from London.

Another way into the hills starts at the Plough, about midway between Ivinghoe and Dunstable. It can on summer weekends be somewhat busy for it leads up to Whipsnade Zoo, an incidental addition to the attractions of the Chilterns. Whipsnade itself appears at first glance more common than village, it is so spread

out around its green. From there a narrow lane leads to Kensworth Church-end, an out-of-the-way corner with a good Georgian
house, a row of cottages probably of Stuart date but now derelict,
and, screened by a row of great limes, a church mainly Norman
except for the fifteenth-century tower. Or there is Studham, also
round a large, swelling common, with a meagre war memorial, a
pleasant and new Methodist church and, nearly out of the village,
its old parish church. Externally a heavily plastered, ungainly
building, it unexpectedly houses an early thirteenth-century nave
which is in two differing styles though apparently built at the
same time. Pevsner suggests that 'an old man and a boy worked
together'; certainly in 1220 when the church was consecrated one-
third of the nave must have appeared to be clinging to the recent
past while the other two-thirds was of the then-modern style (and
recalls Eaton Bray and Edlesborough).

Kensworth and Studham, looking orderly enough now, gave
concern to the government of the day during at least two periods
of their history. It was at Kensworth that during the 1660s John
Bunyan, between spells in Bedford gaol for his religious disobedience, found his steadiest converts. In a house there met one of the
first of Baptist congregations drawn from the villages round about;
during those early days it was customary for people as far afield as
Sundon, Totternhoe and Markyate to gather at Kensworth and
make a day of their sabbath, having 'in fellowship' the meal they
had brought with them between the morning and afternoon
services. In time, as Bunyan's preaching spread, separate congregations were set up, usually in a farm or cottage until the Toleration
Act of 1689 allowed the building of chapels. By then the Baptists'
simple, literal faith had established itself not only in villages but
in Dunstable, Luton, Bedford and St Albans and was becoming
a national movement. By then Bunyan's preaching and person-
ality had reached a much wider audience by way of his *Pilgrim's
Progress*, the greatest allegory in English and an inspiration in time
to millions. Meanwhile there was scarcely a town or village in the
eastern Chilterns that he did not visit ... though it would seem
unlikely, as is sometimes asserted, that the Chiltern hills were
Bunyan's 'delectable mountains'. Essentially a man of simplicity
and humility, Bunyan nevertheless had imagination enough to
envisage a more glorious landscape; but he was, too, a countryman
of his time and, as we saw in the inn at Crowell, ready to delight
in the simpler pleasures of his day. We can perhaps hope that,

though writing in Bedford gaol, he had in mind some Chiltern corner 'where was a den, and I laid me down in that place to sleep; and as I slept I dreamed a dream....'

It was rather after Bunyan's time that Kensworth and Studham joined with other villages round about in a much more secular matter. Many of the villagers were then—and for a full century afterwards—occupied in making straw-plait which was collected and sold in Dunstable and Luton for the making of straw hats; and a remunerative occupation it was for a skilled cottage-wife could earn up to £2 a week, when her labourer husband earned barely ten shillings. But to encourage the lagging wool trade, the government passed an Act favouring the making of wool (i.e. felt) hats—and drew from Kensworth, Studham and their neighbours a petition against the Act; the petition asserted that more than a thousand local families depended on the straw-plait trade, an indication of its importance. The fears that prompted the petition were, however, soon diminished. The wars against France interrupted competition from Italian Leghorn straw hats and a few years later Defoe was able to report that the Chiltern industry was 'wonderfully increased'.

From Studham and Kensworth lanes lead through a quiet countryside to the hollow in which Markyate stands along Watling Street (though the village is now by-passed). Its street, mainly of eighteenth-century houses, needs a few trees to complete it. Somewhere here, perhaps in one of the Georgian houses, was Dr Pitman's school which young William Cowper attended; but recalling the bullying and brutality he there had to suffer which scarred his sensitive nature and led in time to his mental collapse, there is little inclination to identify the house. Perhaps Markyate once attracted odd and dubious characters. A story lingers there about 'wicked Lady Ferrers' who, dressed as a highwayman, robbed benighted travellers on Watling Street. W. B. Gerish, who early in this century made his great collection of Hertfordshire folk lore, suggests that the story may have had some basis in fact ... though we can scarcely hope that now much of the heavier traffic has been diverted along the M 1, 'Lady Ferrers'' ghost, which used to ride along Watling Street on a 'coal-black horse with white fore-feet', will reappear.

Within two miles of Markyate on a hill-top is Flamstead, which in its small compass has a lot to show: seventeenth-century almshouses, a fine Georgian house and an earlier timber-framed one,

and a fourteenth-century church (with Roman brick in its walls as might be expected near Watling Street). Internally the church has Decorated stonework, a fifteenth-century roof, some fourteenth-century wall-paintings with enough to enable the visitor to guess at the figures and some graffiti mainly of curiously triangular faces. All told, Flamstead is a rewarding place to end with and one which to the eye seems much farther than a mile from the modern M 1.

EIGHT

From Watling Street to the Great North Road

Again it must be stressed, even at the risk of tedium, that Icknield is not so rigid a route as cartographers make it appear. The Ways trodden early in its long history were certainly not only those named on the map; so we following Icknield only approximately can, if we feel the need, indulge in an occasional deviation from the map's assertions without worrying that we may be departing from historical accuracy.

Nowhere does this need become more apparent than between Dunstable and Luton. The Icknield Way, as marked, is the A 505 which east of Luton may be an open, bounding road, but before then is anything but inspiring. The map also gives the impression that the thick of Luton's traffic has to be negotiated. In fact, for those who insist on accuracy even to the point of traversing what is now suburban Luton, the Way truly branches off A 505 just after the M 1 under-pass and makes its way along a low ridge between Leagrave and Limbury—that is now-a-days along Stony-gate Road, Roman Road and Icknield Road—to be called Icknield Way as it approaches the New Bedford Road (A 6). The next half-mile has been ploughed up; it went straight for the earthworks of Dray's Ditches on the western flank of Galley Hill. There on the map it regains recognition and its name.

There is a pleasanter way, only possibly a variation of Icknield but certainly ancient. It goes somewhat further north as if to skirt the headstreams of the Lea. It is to be found northeast of Houghton Regis continuing beyond Watling Street the footpath way from Ivinghoe and 'Maiden Bower'. From Houghton to beyond its crossing of the M 1 near Charlton it is a lane, a little-frequented one. Thereafter it becomes a way for the walker, a green lane very like much of the Lower Icknield. It was in medieval times known as

the Salt Way, more anciently as the Ede Way, and was once a minor Roman road. It joins forces with Icknield in the neighbourhood of Dray's Ditches. That somewhat rudimentary earthwork facing southwards appears to have been constructed in Iron Age times as a kind of check-point on both routes and may have been in effect a boundary to a tribal area based on the fort of Ravensburgh Castle on a wooded ridge a mile and a half to its northeast.

From Dray's Ditches Icknield continues as a green lane to Ickleford just north of Hitchin, a distance of nearly seven miles and, with the exception of a brief length where the Hitchin–Barton road intrudes, it is an incredibly rural way. There is scarcely a building on it—just the good fields reaching away on either side: to the wooded crest about Ravensburgh on the north, to the rolling country between Luton and Hitchin on the south. It would be stretching landscape history absurdly far to suggest that the walker can feel that he is almost back in prehistory, but that green road can have changed comparatively little since the last of the cattle-drovers used it in the days before the railways. Not until north of Hitchin does the Way return to the present at Ickleford, whose name is derived from 'Icknield ford' as the walker who persists in rigidly following the map route will find when he has to wade the watercress-choked little River Hiz. Thereafter Icknield continues its green way up to the fragmentary Iron Age fort of Wilbury, where it becomes the main street of Letchworth.

The motorist can share something of this route's quiet by taking the road through Houghton Regis, now rather untidily becoming an offshoot of Dunstable though its church gives a touch of ancient dignity and beyond it is a good village green. As its name tells Houghton Regis was once—back in pre-Conquest times—a large and important royal manor on one corner of which Dunstable was built by Henry I. By bearing right at the church the motorist is soon out in quiet, undulating country with the outskirts of Dunstable disappearing below the skyline and little but lapwings and an occasional kestrel for company. It is not dramatic country, though seen with pale winter sunshine catching the flints in the ploughed fields and with here and there a copse giving a darker touch, it prompts the word pastoral. And it leads, after crossing the M 1, through Sundon and Streatley, both quiet places and each possessing a good church. Internally Sundon's is striking: it looks at first glance as if it has changed little since its first vicar was inducted in 1226, and is on a scale that suggests that Sundon was then a larger

place than now. It has something of a rarity in stone benches that run along each aisle wall, a relic of the time when the congregation had to stand and 'the weakest went to the wall'. The architecture of Streatley church is for the most part a little later (the brick chancel is Victorian).

Three miles east of Streatley during which Galley (once Gallows?) Hill and Warden Hill rise boldly to the south, signposts lead to Lilley and on the way the lane becomes for a half-mile the Icknield Way before another turn leads to Lilley village. It is a long lane of a place, a landowner's village for many of its cottages show the crest of the local family, the Salusburys, whom we shall come across again at Offley. Lilley appears now too open a place to have once known as a resident John Kellerman, the 'last of the Alchemists' who, circa 1820, claimed to be able to make gold from base metal in true medieval fashion. W. B. Gerish, whose collection of local stories has ensured that such odd people will not be forgotten, recorded a visit to Kellerman in 1828 in which the 'alchemist' behaved with disconcerting naturalness; the curious will find the full account in *Hertfordshire Folk Lore*. And despite its present placid appearance, Lilley had an even more disturbing son in James Janeway, a contemporary of Bunyan, who determined that the young of his day should be frightened into his very un-Christian variety of Christianity. In a series of widely read stories he told of children who, after brief 'Holy and Exemplary Lives', were saved from adult temptation leading to the torments of hell by an early demise. (A typical six-year-old hero warns his brothers and sisters of the dangers attendant on a sudden death from choking over their food because they have omitted to say grace.) One of Janeway's favourite maxims for parents was: 'Your child is never too little to go to hell.' Lilley does not deserve to have to own such a character.

Lilley's single street ends on the Luton–Hitchin road and so avoids the necessity of driving through Luton. Perhaps it is a little unfair to dismiss that town so peremptorily, but it must be admitted that, even more so than Dunstable, Luton has little to show for its long history. Old Stone-age tools have been found there. Neolithic people lived at Waulud's Bank in the northwest corner of the borough. The Romans had a settlement between Luton and Leagrave, and the Saxons named the place 'Lygetun', the enclosure by the Lea. At a battle with the Danes in 913, the *Anglo-Saxon Chronicle* records that the Lutonians 'fought against

them [the Danes] and reduced them to full flight and rescued all that they had captured and also a great part of their horse and their weapons'. A castle was built there in King Stephen's reign and another in King John's, erected by his military chief, Fawkes de Breauté ... which adds a quirk to history for that same Fawkes, allegedly a brutal mercenary enjoying almost royal power, also had a hall in London called Fawkes' Hall, corrupted in time to Vauxhall, which name returned to Luton as its best-known product when the town, after centuries as a market town and a spell thriving on the straw-plait trade, became a modern industrial centre. All told, quite a story; those interested will find them in *The Story of Luton* published in 1964 when the town achieved County Borough status. It is a very informative book but a depressing one for the visitor, for only recently have Lutonians tried to preserve some traces from their past—in time to save Waulud's Bank from the developers, and most of the fourteenth-century 'Moat House' at Limbury (once a separate manor); and the parish church, too, which, if it were in a pleasanter situation, might draw more than local and casual visitors. Though originally built about 1200, the church as it stands now is a fine, mainly fifteenth-century building. Inside is a rich collection of monuments and brasses ranging from 1392 to 1526, with the elaborate Wenlock monument the most outstanding; there is also a Decorated Easter Sepulchre in the Chancel, and a fourteenth-century font with a finely carved, contemporary canopy.

Readily accessible from Luton are two places worth noting. On the southern fringe of Luton Airport is 'Someries Castle', truly the twin-towered gatehouse of a fifteenth-century manor-house with a chapel somewhat unexpectedly attached to one side. On the other side were more buildings, though John Leland wrote in 1552 that the house had never been finished. The surviving portion shows an early use of brick.

Across the Lea from Someries Castle is Luton Hoo House in the fine park laid out by 'Capability' Brown. Open sometimes to the public the House can show many attractions: paintings, tapestries, period furniture, a remarkable collection of china, and the Fabergé collection of the last Czar. The House is, however, only in part that designed by Robert Adam for George III's 'dearest friend' and first prime minister, Lord Bute. He settled here after relinquishing office to study botany, a subject more to his liking than politics. The scientific approach was then very much in the air, and Bute

attempted to devise a system of classification to rival that of his Swedish contemporary Linnaeus; more successful, and more to be gratefully remembered, was his persuading the Dowager Princess of Wales to allow the gardens to her palace at Kew to become the Royal Botanic Gardens. The present Luton Hoo House is the result of a thorough remodelling in 1903 after two extensive fires; being the work of the architects of the London Ritz, it is internally impressively Edwardian.

On the map the Luton-Hitchin road looks almost a continuation of the Upper Icknield, but no evidence has been found that it was in use before Saxon times. If the one village along it, Offley, truly remembers the name of Offa the Great, his Mercian majesty would seem to have chosen a somewhat out-of-the-way place for his residence.

Standing high just before a sharp fall to the gap in which Hitchin stands, Offley is a pleasantly open village well endowed with inns: the Green Man at the cross-roads appears to date from about 1680, the Red Lion looks older inside than its Victorian slate roof suggests. Between the two is the church, an odd mixture of late thirteenth century and mid-eighteenth century. The nave arcade has 'stiff-leaved' capitals typical of so-called Early English work, the aisle windows are Late Perp.; but the chancel, whatever it may have been originally, was rebuilt about 1750 by Sir Thomas Salusbury in the classical style then in vogue—though in the odd recess for the east window it looks as if some attempt was made at a compromise between the pointed arch of the Gothic and the round arch favoured in the eighteenth century. Clearly the chancel was designed to display the monuments to the Salusburys and their relations; and again we meet that uncertainty that has already been noticed about eighteenth-century and later monuments ... though in that to Sir Thomas and Lady Sarah Salusbury there is a personal touch that relieves its classical formality. The two large figures stand before an oak tree, Sir Thomas offering his wife a wreath. The story tells that the way of love did not run smoothly for them. Soon after Sir Thomas and the widowed Sarah King (née Burroughs) became engaged, a lovers' quarrel parted them ... until while walking separately in the grounds of nearby Wellbury a sudden shower caused them to shelter under the same tree where they renewed their engagement. The scene is depicted as their memorial, and the wreath he is offering her is appropriately of myrtle, the wedding flower.

Down an abrupt hill and three miles ahead is Hitchin; but on Halfway Hill a lane leading northwestwards offers a glance at Pirton if time allows. It is an intriguing little place, a series of looping byroads—'streets' is much too urban a word—with houses and cottages in a surprising variety clustering along them. Pevsner singles out three for special mention: the gabled, brick-and-timber Hammond's Farm, Rectory Farm mainly of stone and of early Tudor appearance, and Old Hall, dated 1609; but for those who wander around the village there are a dozen lesser ones, some timber-framed, some warm brick, and all of them attractive. The village, as the many lanes and tracks leading to it suggest, was once an important place; and rising near the church, originally of the twelfth century, is the tree-covered motte and earthen bailey of the castle which was built, probably soon after the Conquest, to command the Hitchin gap. The motte is known locally as 'Toot Hill', a name suggesting that the mound existed before the Conqueror's time and that the Saxons had used it as a look-out point.

Back across Icknield to Hitchin and Letchworth and Baldock. Though separate towns, all three shared for a thousand years a similar experience, for the area on which they stand has provided finds from the Bronze Age, was comparatively intensively settled during the Iron Age, and saw much of the Romans, Letchworth becoming, like Dunstable, a recognised posting station and headquarters of the local policing forces. They are now very different in appearance and the differences make interesting contrasts.

Hitchin now appears the oldest. The streets about its market place have retained a medieval pattern and can show several houses and shops which tell of at least a Tudor origin—Pevsner suspects that some may be a century older. Their half-timbered overhangs add to the late medieval impression while those of more recent date —mainly seventeenth and eighteenth century and square-faced and trim—are in proportion. Among these older streets is the church, the one true 'wool church' of the Chilterns. Large and impressively battlemented, it proclaims to the visitor entering by the fine south porch the origin of its splendour: the arms of the Staple of Calais are still prominently displayed, a five-hundred-year-old reminder of the days when Hitchin's rich wool merchants remodelled the thirteenth-century building they had inherited. Inside it has the spaciousness and the dignity, and the lightness from the wider windows, that are characteristic of Perpendicular Gothic—though some of the earlier church, such as the nave arcade and the roof

to the north aisle, were incorporated in the later building. Everywhere one looks—up at the nave roof, at the many brasses, at the screens, the font, the pulpit, at some of the stalls with their 'poppyheads'—the fifteenth-century richness is there. The church epitomises the wool-based prosperity of late medieval England.

Letchworth is utterly different, the first product of twentieth-century town planning. It was the earliest expression of that humane and practical visionary Ebenezer Howard who, in 1898, published the then-new idea of planning industrial towns rather than, as ever since the Industrial Revolution, letting them just happen with random siting of factories and works, with random areas of land turned into slabs of terraced streets for workers' families and, often apart, avenues of more impressive detacheds for the well-to-do (which had often long before Howard's time become lodging houses shared by several families). Howard asserted that a town should be planned, the industrial area apart from the residential streets, the shopping centre and the community buildings placed where they would best serve local needs, areas left as open spaces for everyone to enjoy. And the town as a whole should be a unit, self-supplying with work and needs. Such ideals, still new at the turn of the century, can be seen put into reality in Letchworth from 1903 onwards. To judge it the visitor should not think of what has happened since but what had been done before. It may be that, as Pevsner says, the major buildings are a little inadequate; it may be that the 'cottagy-suburban' type of semi-detached, having long become familiar elsewhere, tends to be a little insistent; but even the least architecturally inclined visitor must appreciate the fresh greenness of Letchworth in the generously treed open spaces, along the streets, in the gardens. Many later council estates, 'garden cities', and New Towns are still benefiting from Howard's vision.

Baldock is again different. Though its church is for the most part a century earlier than Hitchin's the centre of the town appears rather more recent. The impression is of a town which thrived on the stage-coaches and the increasing traffic of their day, and being on the Great North Road thrived more than the majority of such towns. It is mainly Georgian, neat, quietly dignified, and brick—though here and there a few earlier, timber-framed houses (one dated 1632) have survived.

Baldock church, which Pepys thought 'very beautiful', is mainly fourteenth century though most of its windows were enlarged a century later. It is for its period rather plain; the Decorated work

is mostly in the corbels and the little figures between the arches. It has contrived to keep its fifteenth-century screen, also simple in design for the period, and a number of brasses dating from about 1400 to 1530 and including a rare one to a forester.

The name Baldock has intriguing possibilities. The Place-Name people, pointing out that it was 'Baldac' in 1168, suggest that this French form of what is now Baghdad was applied to the buildings of the Knights Templar who then owned the manor. To find so English a town owing its name to so romantic an origin is surprising. But recently this derivation has been queried, notably by G. L. Evans in 'Hertfordshire Past and Present' (No. 8, 1968). He points out that 'Baldac' was earlier 'Baldoc', the round oak; he also draws attention to the place-name Lannock, once part of the manor of Baldock and surviving in a hamlet a mile to the south, which was formerly 'Langen-ok', the long (tall) oak; while Stevenage still further south was once 'Stivenach', the stiff [firm] oak ... which hints of the possibility of directions for travellers along the Great North Road before the days of signposts: go from the firm oak to the long oak, and from there make for the round oak....

At Baldock we are at the end of this stretch of Icknield; but before leaving perhaps there is time for remembering a few of the notable people who have lived hereabouts. Hitchin has produced many—they can be found in Reginald Hine's *History of Hitchin* and *Hitchin Worthies,* classics of local history. The best-known by name was George Chapman, though he would have preferred to be remembered for some of his own prodigious writings rather than for the much later sonnet he inadvertently inspired when John Keats felt 'like some watcher of the skies. When a new planet swims into his ken; Or like stout Cortez...' For this George Chapman is that contemporary of such giants as Shakespeare, Marlowe, Ben Jonson and Edmund Spenser who is known to all but the very well-informed of us only from 'On first looking into Chapman's Homer'. But for Keats even his individual and Elizabethanised translation would have long been forgotten ... though there is a story which links it directly with the Hitchin neighbourhood and provides what must be the literary event not of its century but of all time. For Chapman's determination to undertake the translation of Homer —which took him thirteen years and for which his Greek was not, strictly speaking, adequate—arose not from a love of Greek authors or from the hope that it would prove a best-seller or even pay the rent. It was nothing so mundane. It was, as Chapman himself later

told, in response to the command of Homer's ghost that he undertook the immense work, and Homer had even journeyed from a
warm and colourful Elysium above the mountains of Greece to
the humbler and cooler 'heights over Hitchin' to communicate his
wishes. The Chilterns can have witnessed few stranger meetings.

Baldock, too, once knew a writer who, like Chapman, is remembered, and remembered as gratefully for his association with
another better-known author. It is to John Smith, once rector of
Baldock, that we owe Pepys' diary. Written in a private shorthand
(and at times of more intimate confession using a mixture of Latin,
French and Spanish), the diary was for a full century after Pepys'
death left untouched and unregarded ... until early in the 1800s
John Smith, then an undergraduate at St John's, Cambridge, tried
his hand at code-breaking and, after three years of intensive work,
gave to the public the famous collection of gossip, information,
personal likes and dislikes, comings and goings, the whole vivid
impression of Charles II's England through which runs the very
human character of Pepys himself.

The region southwards of the length of Icknield just covered is
difficult to describe adequately. Little is the word that first comes
to mind; it is a land of little hills, little valleys, little hamlets,
little woods, little fields. This is not to imply that there is a meagre-
ness about it or a triviality; it is quiet, undramatic and green with
many copses, and possesses a seemingly endless variety of view
though never giving those wide vistas that come when the crest
ends at the rim of the plain.

It is essentially a region won from forest. So, too, is much of
the Chiltern country; but here it looks the result of more random
and more individual effort. To the east, the wide fields suggest
communal working, as if all the workers of largish villages com-
bined to make collective and determined efforts to clear their land
almost to its boundaries; to the west the smaller fields often limited
by the sudden slopes appear to have originated from their villages.
But in the region south of the Luton–Hitchin road one can imagine
family groups venturing into untamed forest, building a rough
home there and then clearing, through several seasons, a few patches
of land for their needs. There are so few villages hereabouts. Whitwell, probably now the largest, has never attained the position of a
parish centre. Kimpton, similarly along a shallow valley, must
until the last century have been only a small place. And as for

the rest—Preston, King's Walden, St Paul's Walden, Ayot St Lawrence—they are, or were until recently, hardly villages at all, just groups of church, manor-house, perhaps a home farm and a few labourers' cottages, while spread over their parishes are a dozen even smaller hamlets, 'Ends' suggesting later clearances, 'Greens' hinting of squatting on a fragment of grazing land.

The road pattern fits such a random, individual winning of the land. The lanes twist and turn and climb and tilt as if they hardly knew where they were making for. There was once a Roman road running through the region from near Wheathampstead (where there was a late Iron Age 'oppidum') to the Hitchin area; but even the thorough and on-the-ground 'Viatores' have found little more of it than a few random stretches. It seems likely that in the early days of Anglo-Saxon England when the Hicce were settling the neighbourhood of Hitchin and the Waeclingas were settling near St Albans (and incidentally leaving a corruption of their name to Watling Street) and the Breahings were settling around Braughing, this central region was left to revert to forest. Or perhaps, as the first syllable of Walden comes from the Saxon word applied to the Britons, the area was merely left to the 'natives'. On the other hand its villagers may have left when in Alfred the Great's time the nearby River Lea formed part of the boundary between English and Danish England: who with plenty of good land available would struggle to clear the forest from land which was likely to be fought over? By the Domesday Book, however, the area appears to have become more settled though the high figures for 'pannage' (masts for feeding pigs) implies that it was still a very wooded land.

Any route through such an area is bound to be meandering. There are alternative approaches. One leads southwards from Offley to King's Walden whose church, originally thirteenth century, until recently possessed a graffito of a Latin text in beautiful medieval script; but the lintel on which it had been scratched has been remodelled, though some compensation may be found by looking at the south, inner side of the tower arch where is another graffito, this time of a jester playing the medieval forerunner of the bagpipe, a shawm. Or one can go southeastwards from Letchworth, through Willian with its little green and its cottages gathered around its mainly fifteenth-century church (with some good 'poppy-heads'), and on to hill-top Great Wymondley. This village once had a castle; the motte can be seen near the

church which is still largely Norman and still has, remarkably, its apse. Delamere House here is sometimes said to have been one of Cardinal Wolsey's residences; it is clearly of nearly a century after his time though Wolsey is known to have stayed at times in the village. Either route the traveller, if literary-minded, should make for Preston.

At first glance Preston is a mere hamlet around a green still retaining its well and well-head. It is sometimes visited for adjoining Temple Dinsley which in Domesday Book was the centre of a manor (which, as the name tells, became in the twelfth century the property of the Knights Templar), later an early eighteenth-century house, and was in 1908 remodelled by Sir Edwin Lutyens in the style that made him an outstanding architect during the early years of this century. But for those in the know, Preston is to be visited for one who lived there during the 1760s in the castle now only remembered in the name of Castle Farm. He was in life Captain Robert Hinde, but it is not in life or by that name that he is remembered—and as one of the greatest of comic characters in English Literature.

His castle at Preston was Hinde's own creation. He had inherited an undistinguished country house; but he, the epitome of the old soldier and a naturally robust and thorough-going character, needed something more impressive as the setting for one who had served His Majesty—probably with more gusto than efficiency—in the wars against the French. His house had to be remodelled to suit his military prowess; it had to have battlements and turrets and a portcullis, and to be encircled with outer earthen defences. It had also to be equipped and peopled suitably. A battery of eight guns —seven small and a large one standing before them—greeted visitors. Hinde's servants were fitted out with uniforms—we must assume that he had kept his own from the Seven Years' War—so that any and every one passing by should know that there lived one of His Majesty' officers (even if now retired).

Hinde was not, however, the man to keep his military display to himself. He was, above all, a generous man. On every possible occasion—a royal birthday, the anniversary of a British victory, whenever the military news seemed to justify acknowledgement— his battery of eight guns announced to the neighbourhood that Captain Hinde was about to begin one of his patriotic perform- ances. His servants in their uniforms, himself at their head, the whole entourage rode into Hitchin town with 'martial trumpetings

and huzzas'. There in the market place Hinde announced to the people of Hitchin the event which had prompted the display—and we are told that the assembled townsfolk enjoyed these occasions almost as much as Hinde did.

Such performances came in time to be known throughout a wider area and reached as far as Kimpton Hoo, whose owner Thomas Brand (later Lord Dacre) was a friend of Laurence Sterne, then starting work on a new and, as it turned out, very original novel. Hearing of the activities of Captain Hinde, Sterne was quick to see the possibilities in such a character. One day he and Brand rode over to Preston where, in the person of Captain Hinde, Sterne met Tristram Shandy's immortal 'Uncle Toby'.

A mile to the east and hidden in a small wood is a very different place of pilgrimage: the ruin of Minsden chapel. The thick ivy which until recently shrouded the place and damaged the fabric has now been cleared away; but, even so, there is little of architectural interest in the fragmentary walls and now-shapeless window and door openings of what had been the fourteenth-century chapel serving the few villagers left of the 'Minlesden' of the Domesday Book. It appears to have been in occasional use up to the early 1700s, the last recorded service being a marriage in 1738 which was rendered more than usually memorable by masonry falling dangerously near the officiating curate during the ceremony. By then the Anglican Church all but ignored the place; the occasional congregations were more of Baptists drawn there to hear a successor to Bunyan.

It is not, however, for its history or its architecture that people are drawn to what is left of Minsden chapel. It is the memory of Reginald Hine, the outstanding local historian. But his works are not merely history; through them runs Hine's feeling for the town and its setting. And prominent in that setting was Minsden chapel. When writing of his friend Frederick Griggs, in his day a notable etcher, Hine tells how, as young men, they would often visit the chapel and sometimes spend several hours there while Griggs sketched the crumbling walls and Hine experienced the strange fascination of the place. Hine, of course, found out all he could of its history, its mysteries, its alleged ghosts; he leased the chapel from the Church authorities for his lifetime and asked that he might be buried there. A stone in the small, ruined chancel marks his grave.

Southward is St Paul's Walden, the fourteenth-century church of which, like Offley's, had its chancel rebuilt in the eighteenth

century and in a more lavish style; but it has contrived to retain a beautiful medieval Virgin and Child in the glass of its west window. Walden Bury, a little to the south, is the birthplace of Queen Elizabeth the Queen Mother. Farther on is Whitwell, a laneside village with two or three pleasant pubs—though the sign of the Eagle and Child has got the wrong story—and then Kimpton, another long place with the parish church for both villages and notable mainly for its ancient woodwork including some good 'poppy-heads'.

From Kimpton two lanes each offer a literary association. Southeastwards is Ayot St Lawrence with G.B.S.'s home for forty years at Shaw's Corner, left at his request to the National Trust. The house itself, the former rectory, is architecturally unremarkable and its setting in the restrained Hertfordshire countryside seems hardly in keeping with one who for half a century taunted, cajoled, urged and stung the play-going public into questioning its placidly accepted assumptions on almost every aspect of human society. Somehow at first glance Shaw's Corner, in its determination to keep his surroundings as he knew them, tends to appear rather too ordinary for so extraordinary a character. The desk he worked at, the encyclopaedias near at hand, the typewriter his secretary used, the filing cabinets—these could have been those of many a lesser writer; and the portraits and mementoes we might expect, and perhaps in this rural setting the collection of hats and walking sticks; and, remembering his beginnings as a music critic, the Bechstein on which he played fragments from his favourite operas. Little of these seem at first to suggest the man. It is not until we take a more careful look—particularly at his library ranging across a far wider knowledge than we can recollect from his plays—that we begin to glimpse Shaw. And then we also begin to realise that he was not truly quite as he often appeared in the public's recollection. The wit of his plays, the repartee he put into the mouths of his characters, and the quick dart of his speech (as we imagine it from his writings and from newspaper reports) these which we have come to assume to have been almost spontaneous—intuitive rather than cultivated—were, in fact, products of an extremely well-informed and very orderly mind, as well as a very keen one. Indeed Shaw's Corner leaves an impression not of an impulsive, quick-fire genius but of a very disciplined one.

At Ayot St Lawrence linger some memories that we, recalling his tart, highly critical public persona, may not expect. Shaw took a personal interest in many a village happening and many a local

can tell of the help he gave them. Those who would begin to understand Shaw the man as well as Shaw the playwright could do well to start there.

Ayot St Lawrence has another sight and another story for visitors in its two churches. The medieval one, which claimed association with Rahere, the founder of Bart's Hospital, was used as a quarry for the new church, built in 1778/9 by Sir Lyonel Lyle. This was designed by Nicholas Revett, a protagonist of the 'Greek Revival' and an associate of Sir Francis Dashwood and his 'Society of Dilettanti'. One cannot help suspecting that Sir Lyonel, a London business man turned country gentleman, wished to impress. When applying to 'rebuild' the old church he maintained that to keep it in repair would cost the then-large sum of £600 which he pleaded was too great a cost; but he spent over £6,000 on his own new church. And he insisted that it was designed to suit his wishes. So that the east front, which faced his house, might form a fitting 'prospect', he had the altar placed at the west end; he also compelled the villagers to use a long roundabout path so that as they went to church they would remain invisible from his windows. And the main east front had to be suitably impressive with a large portico and on either side a colonnade ending in an open pavilion. These pavilions, apparently merely decorative, seem to have had some special significance for Sir Lyonel; on his instructions he was buried outside one and his wife outside the other. This curious instruction prompted local gossip that, their marriage having been far from a happy one, Sir Lyonel and Lady Lyle determined that the Church which had joined them in life should in death permanently part them ... or perhaps the story was prompted by some villager's annoyance at the unnecessarily long walk he had to make each Sunday.

Southwestwards from Kimpton lies Mackerye End with its cluster of cottages and its Stuart great house for those who prefer a gentler literary figure than Shaw. There, after an interval of forty years, came Charles Lamb and his sister Mary (whom he calls his cousin 'Bridget' to avoid recognition by the readers of *Elia*), to revisit the scene of a childhood happening and perhaps to renew the acquaintance of their Gladman kinsfolk there:

> By a somewhat circuitous route, taking the noble park of Luton in our way from Saint Albans, we arrived at the spot of our anxious curiosity about noon. The sight of the old farmhouse,

though every trace of it was effaced from my recollection, affected me with a pleasure I had not experienced for many a year.... Bridget's was more a waking bliss than mine, for she easily remembered her old acquaintance again, some altered features, of course, a little grudged at. At first, indeed, she was ready to dis-believe for joy; but the scene soon reconfirmed itself in her affec-tions, and she traversed every outpost of the mansion, to the woodhouse, the orchard, the place where the pigeon-house had stood (house and birds were alike flown) with a breathless im-patience of recognition, which was more pardonable perhaps than decorous at the age of fifty-odd...

The only thing left was to get into the house, and that was a difficulty which to me singly would have been insurmountable; for I am terribly shy in making myself known to strangers and out-of-date kinsfolk. Love stronger than scruple winged my cousin in without me; but she soon returned with a creature that might have sat for a sculptor for the image of Welcome. It was the youngest of the Gladmans; who, by marriage with a Bruton, had become the mistress of the old mansion. A comely brood are the Brutons. Six of them, females, were noted as the handsomest young women in the county. But this adopted Bruton, in my mind, was better than they all—more comely.

Those slender ties that prove slight as gossamer in the rending atmosphere of a metropolis bind faster, as we found it, in hearty, homely, loving Hertfordshire. In five minutes we were as thor-oughly acquainted as if we had been born and bred up together ... The fatted calf was made ready, or rather was already so, as if in anticipation of our coming; and, after an appropriate glass of native wine, never let me forget with what honest pride this hospitable cousin made us proceed to Wheathampstead, to introduce us (as some newfound rarity) to her mother and sister Gladmans.... When I forget this, then may my country cousins forget me.

Which would seem—as the A 6 is conveniently near at hand—an appropriate point to end this section of the Chilterns ... though nearby Wheathampstead's rising street has many a house in it that Charles and Mary Lamb would have passed, and a fine, mainly thirteenth-century church, and a half-mile to the east traces of the ramparts of the Iron Age fortification, surrounding something of a town, that Julius Caesar's men stormed....

NINE

From Baldock to Royston

For the nine miles from Baldock to Royston the Icknield Way, as mapped, is the main road (A 505), and there is not a village along it. There must once have been several if the round barrows along the route are any guide to the local population from Bronze Age times. And these are the survivals from what once must have been a considerable number; the solitary barrow on Highley Hill, for example, was once one of the 'Nine Barrows', while about the cluster on Therfield Heath near Royston are traces of others.

This dearth of villages is curious. Through most of its length the Icknield's villages are sited just off the actual Ways, but of the eight within range of the Baldock-Royston road only small Bygrave is within a mile of Icknield; the other seven stand well out in the low, swelling fields to the north or three miles away on top of the crest to the south. And neither Baldock nor Royston existed during the first five or six centuries of those villages' lives. No doubt there is an explanation for this apparent avoidance of Icknield though as yet local history and archaeology are uninformative.

For the motorist this means that Icknield is here an open, undulating road making its direct way between wide fields which to the south rise up to a more defined crest blurred with woods. From the spur of Gallows Hill—a reminder of the once-customary gruesome method of publishing the news that justice had been done—the road more closely follows the escarpment. The Romans used much of this way though for the first two miles out of Baldock they asserted a more direct line a half-mile of which, as a raised 'agger', can be seen crossing the fields south of Bygrave. There the modern road follows the slightly curving course of the prehistoric Way.

For the walker there is about two miles north the quiet and archaeologically puzzling green lane of Ashwell Street. Stretches of

it are judged by the 'Viatores' to have been Romanised, at least banked in places though apparently never paved. It would seem to have been in existence as a link way between settlements about Baldock and Hitchin with those around Royston at least in Iron Age times so that, in spite of the persistence of the title 'street'—which usually denotes a Roman road and has been in use from at least Henry II's time—the walker is in effect following a continuation of the Lower Icknield. If he is of an imaginative turn he can people the five quiet green miles beyond Ashwell with any beings from Iron-agers to cattle drovers of a century ago. Ashwell Street has known them all.

The first two miles linking Ashwell village with the Roman road that became the Great North Road are a little uncertain. The 'Viatores', thorough as ever, offer two beginnings both leading to Ashwell but both a little hazy on the way. The easier for the walker (and for the motorist following much the same direction) is the lane through Newnham though strictly speaking that village lies between the two early routes.

Newnham is a rather out-of-the-way place, and the first sight of its little green flanked by definitely twentieth-century houses—of circa 1925 vintage but better than many of that time—is unexpected. For an older impression it is necessary to approach along the lane from Caldecote (whose church and few houses look almost as if they have been dropped in the swelling cornfields a few centuries back and nearly forgotten since). Newnham is in fact old enough to have been 'Neuham' in the Domesday Book. Opposite its church, small and ancient, is a solid, square Georgian house and a row of cottages made out of what was in Stuart times the manor's malting house, a reminder that hereabouts and for many miles spreading southwards was—and still is—the great barley-growing area for London's ale. For those who have read Reginald Hine's works on the history of Hitchin, Newnham church could be a place of pilgrimage; a tapestry in late medieval style is his memorial there.

Mention of Domesday Book recalls that hereabouts William's victorious army reappeared en route for London after its sojourn farther north. Caldecote and Bygrave both suffered a diminution of their value, as did also many of the villages further south; and another line of spoliation is to be found to the east. It seems that the Norman forces, apparently in two columns, moved southwards through the gaps in which Baldock and Royston were later to be built to converge on the Hertford neighbourhood.

Two straightish miles east of Newnham (for the lane now follows the Romanised Way) is Ashwell, which apparently saw little of the Norman soldiery; but it has seen much else. At first glance it appears still a late medieval town, there are so many timber-framed houses with their plastered overhangs—though in fact there are in its brief streets also seventeenth- and eighteenth-century houses, one the humble beginnings in 1681 of the Merchant Taylors' School. Adding to the medieval impression are the gabled Town House (now a delightful local museum) and the black-and-white St John's Guild Hall and, matching in appearance if perhaps not quite as old, the Rose and Crown.

Appropriately Ashwell has one of the most striking churches hereabouts. The lofty, four-staged tower, topped with the narrow spire known as 'Hertfordshire spike' or flèche, is the oldest part; it was built a decade before the Black Death struck ... and is here remembered in a Latin graffito on the internal north wall. A translation reads:

> The beginning of the plague was in 1350 minus one ... wretched, fierce, violent, the dregs of the populace live to tell the tale. At the end of the second [pestilence] a mighty wind: this year Maurus thunders in the heavens 1361.

The reference to the second outbreak of the plague is a reminder that at intervals right up to 1665 England knew the recurring horror. The storm which occurred on St Maurus's Day, 15 January 1361, is known to have destroyed many buildings, uprooted trees and caused several deaths.

The fine tower of Ashwell church, however, survived and in spite of all that the place had suffered the body of the church was built between 1365 and 1380. It is all on a magnificent scale for the small town, though it must be admitted that the lack of decoration and the absence of fittings and monuments of note leave a slightly austere impression.

For those who delight in the curious there are other graffiti in this church, including a Latin phrase: 'Drunkenness breaks whatever wisdom makes', and one of a large church which may represent Old St Paul's or perhaps Westminster Abbey, which had the patronage of Ashwell church during the later Middle Ages.

The walker passes scarcely a building on the five-mile stretch along the green lane of Ashwell Street. For the motorist the roughly

parallel lane goes through Steeple Morden—which lost its steeple in 1633 and the replacement of 1866 over the south porch is hardly impressive enough to justify the distinctive name—and Litlington, where was discovered in 1828 a Roman crematorium (and those who wish to see the urns and vases will have to visit Cambridge Geological Museum), and in 1936 a large Roman villa. Its church is notable for the carvings on the hood moulds, especially that of the 'bridled woman' whose expression suggests that she was capable of saying more than she ought to. Both villages have some pleasant cottages, some thatched, some pantiled, but unfortunately some now roofed with corrugated iron.

On to Bassingbourn-cum-Kneesworth, which ends on the Roman road to Royston. Once the home of Blanche of Lancaster, John of Gaunt's first wife for whom Chaucer wrote his *Boke of the Duchesse*, Bassingbourn deserves to be better known; it deserves, too, to attract residents willing to undertake the restoration of some of its older cottages. The main street leading past the church has trees along its wide verge giving the place a green openness where once market stalls stood, for Bassingbourn like Ashwell was a market town of some local importance. The church is not quite on the scale of Ashwell's and its tower is Victorian; but its chancel, 'a complete and remarkably personally designed piece of Dec architecture', Pevsner says, is finer than that of any church hereabouts. Built in the decade before the Black Death, it sums up on a small scale the triumph of the appropriately named Decorated architecture just before the Europe-wide calamity ended it.

In this church, too, is a monument rare for the feeling it conveys. It is dated 1647, of the time when, as has already been noted, the prone, praying figures of medieval times and the kneeling, praying figures of Tudor fashion had been discarded, and the more worldly and posed monuments of the eighteenth century were still to come. On a black marble slab lies the white, partly shrouded figure of young Henry Butler in a relaxed pose. He might be sleeping. The unforced naturalness awakens sympathy; the surrounding marble blackness, large in comparison with the forlorn figure, gives a strange impression of the loneliness of death.

Bassingbourn is one of those places distinguished by the survival of much of its Churchwardens' Accounts. They tell of the great days of the town when, on St Margaret's Day 1511, a play of the 'holy martir seynt georg' was held to raise money for the church, and of the 'Church Ales' (the medieval equivalent of sales of work though

rather less decorous) which in 1497 produced more than £14 towards the cost of bringing a new treble bell from London.

It would be fitting if Royston, the last of the Icknield towns, were the most attractive. Its origin is alleged to be more appealing than many a town that 'just happened'. Camden, writing about 1580, tells the story:

> Upon the very edge of the county of Hertfordshire to the north standeth Royston, a town of much note but not ancient, having arisen since the Norman Conquest. For in those days there was a famous lady named Roysia (by some supposed to have been Countess of Norfolk) who erected a cross upon the roadside in this place (which was thought in that age to be a pious work to put passengers in mind of Christ's Passion) from thence many years called Royses Cross.

The place was certainly of post-Conquest foundation and from the twelfth century was known in various spellings as 'Royes Cross'. To track down the origin of the story is, however, complicated by there having been in early medieval times at least three ladies named Roisia holding nearby manors though perhaps the likeliest candidate is the wife of Eustace de Merc who 'built a cloyster there'; the foundation of his Augustinian house was confirmed by Papal Bull in 1184.

Some remains of the monastery are incorporated in Royston church, but the building has experienced a complex history. It was apparently partly destroyed following the Reformation, a portion was used as the parish church, was added to 'at some uncertain period', and finally in late Victorian times remodelled in the Early English style—and that restoration was carried out more convincingly than many of its period. For the curious, Pevsner outlines the various contributions, though he has to admit that 'fresh detail research is needed', particularly as some architectural items from the earlier building have been incorporated in the present large and not unimpressive one.

Royston's sight is, however, not its church but its cave. Its discovery in 1742 caused a more-than-local stir. Some workmen making a hole for a post for a market stall found the going unexpectedly hard and, scraping away the earth, saw a large mill-stone; on lifting this they were surprised to discover a cavity—the top entrance to the so-called cave. Investigation showed not only a cavern hollowed out

of the chalk widening to about 17 feet in diameter at the bottom, but also there, some 28 feet down, a female human skeleton. As if that was insufficient of a find, a multitude of crude carvings festooned the rough walls. Some of these were seen to be of Biblical subjects; others would seem to be of legendary figures. All are clearly not the work of skilled sculptors of any age.

Guesses and assumptions about the origin and use of the cave—which could conceivably have originated as a Neolithic flint mine—started at once. The bones were assigned to 'Lady Roisia' on the authority of Stukeley, the leading contemporary antiquarian; the religious motifs of the carvings prompted suggestions of an 'oratory', of a Romano-British place of Christian worship which was abandoned and covered in when the heathen Saxons appeared, of a secret meeting-place for those who took the considerable risk of disagreeing with Henry VIII's religious views. Such guessing has continued. Meanwhile, in 1790 a local builder to provide work for his labourers and profit for himself cut the present passage-entry. The cave is a place to visit for those who like to exercise their imagination for, as yet, no certainty as to its purpose or period has limited speculation.

Royston also possesses a few remains, very much altered since it was first built in 1603, of the hunting box James I founded there (and called locally the 'Old Palace'). It seems His Scottish Majesty was much impressed with the place as he journeyed southwards to claim his cousin's throne. And well he might have been for Royston did him proud: 'drawing neere the Towne ... he was received by that worthy knight Sir Edward Denny, High Shiriffe of Hartfordshire, attended upon by a goodly companie of proper men, being in number seven score, suitably apparelled, their liveries blew coates with sleeves parted in the middest, buttoned behinde in jerkin fashion, and white doublets, and hats and feathers, and all of them mounted on horses with red saddles. Sir Edward after his humble dutie done, presented his Majestie with a gallant horse, a riche saddle, and furniture correspondent to the same, being of great value, which his Majestie accepted very graciously....'

Within a year James had made his hunting box at Royston his chief country residence, returning there whenever the royal duties would allow (and sometimes to the annoyance of his Ministers when they would not), 'esteeming it beyond all places for ye hunting of ye hare, and yt ye hares here were more stoute and ye sents lay better than in any other places'. However, his Majesty was soon critical of

the locals, complaining of the 'spoile and destruction of our game ... we resolve for the time to come to withstand and punish such boldness and contempt, and especiallie and particularlie near unto Royston....' And the locals for their part appear to have found little to respect in their royal resident—in appearance and manner few kings have been less regal—and were dropping hints that they would not mind if he settled elsewhere. Meanwhile, since the King resorted to Royston whenever he could, events were taking place there of more than local significance: in November 1604 Hertford puritans petitioned for freedom of worship and drew a royal determination that the Anglican Church should be predominant in James's new realm; in October 1605 Lord Monteagle sent there a letter concerning a projected attempt to blow up the Houses of Parliament, and so condemned Guy Fawkes and others; in December 1624 the French ambassadors visited Royston to negotiate the fateful marriage of Prince Charles to Henrietta Maria.

Charles when he became king also stayed frequently in the Royston 'Palace' until the events leading up to the Civil War left him less and less time for recreation. His last visit was in June 1647 as a prisoner of Parliament's army, which was at the time defying Parliament (some of whose members were attempting to do a deal with the King behind the army's back). When, a month later, the army ignored Parliament's orders and moved southwards, it was to occupy London and so set the stage for the last act of King Charles's life.

For all its history Royston gives the impression rather of an eighteenth-century town. Though some of its narrower streets suggest the medieval pattern, the buildings can show little that is older than Georgian. Even the former Dead Street, said to have earned its gruesome name during the Black Death, has long been the noncommittal Back Street. Royston looks another of those towns that thrived on the passing traffic from 1700 onwards; and also no doubt on its market, too, for as Leland had written in 1543, though 'the towne it self is but of mene building', the market 'is meruelusly frequented, espetially with corne'.

The country south of this stretch of Icknield has some surprises. The lanes leading to the first villages, set on hill-tops, cross initially the southerly continuation of the undulating cornfields about Ashwell and Bassingbourn. One expects beyond the ridge will lie a land of small fields interspersed with woods, typical of so much of the Chilterns; but instead there are quite wide stretches of open fields

with low hedges—they have been low for generations and are not the product of recent 'grubbing up' the wisdom of which has been questioned in adjoining East Anglia. Here and there woods persist, but not infrequently—such as around Buntingford and Walkern and Watton-at-Stone—the passer-by will gain more open views than he might have expected, the fields rising and swelling over gentler, smoother hills. It is hare and lapwing country. No doubt for centuries as much of it as possible has been used for the essential barley; and befitting such an occupation the villages tend to be more compact, though many have during their long life sprouted later 'Ends'.

Take, for example, the lane that leaves the Baldock–Bishop's Stortford road (A 507) as it begins to climb the ridge and wanders through Clothall to Weston. Clothall itself is a small place, a group of cottages about its inn along a loop road, and a few larger houses about the abrupt little hill on which stands the church (and it is worth glancing into for the stained glass of its east window: mainly fifteenth-century with 'medallions' showing the Virgin and several saints set in a delightful pattern of leaves and birds). Weston on the ridge is larger. The main village is set about two small greens, almost adjoining, and looks as if Weston was once a more important place. There are many pleasant houses, the older of them in the traditional plaster and timber and some thatched—for hereabouts flint was little used, and brick and tile were often reserved for the larger buildings and the chimneys, as witness Weston's bold ones.

The clue to Weston's comparative size is to be found in its church, if the visitor can overlook the Victorian brick chancel clumsily imitating Norman, and the rather bulky tower. Inside waits a surprise, for the tower rests on the fine, sombre Norman arches of a church that had been planned on an impressive scale. It was built about 1180 by that religious-cum-military order, the Knights Templar. At the height of their power, early in the twelfth century, they acquired extensive landed property; but with declining interest in crusading, support for them dwindled, and in 1308 Edward II was able to seize their property in anticipation of the papal abolition of the Order in 1312. It seems that thereafter their church at Weston served as the parish church. In the fifteenth century its nave was rebuilt, out of proportion to the earlier work, but it still retains its contemporary roof supported on corbels with a variety of those strange half-human faces that medieval sculptors seemed to think essential to a church.

24. *Watermill, Mapledurham*

SURVIVALS

25. *Dovecote, Little Gaddesden*

26. *The Great North Road at Baldock*

CHILTERN TOWNSCAPES

27. *The Aylesbury Road at Wendover*

All told, Weston appears to be one of those villages which should
one day have its story written—particularly as it has the additional
distinction of having once provided accommodation for the local
Robin Hood. Known as Jack o' Legs, he was allegedly a giant; two
stones in Weston churchyard over fourteen feet apart were said
to mark his head and feet in his grave. He lived in a cave near the
village and 'was a great Robber, but a generous one, for he plundered the Rich to feed the Poor. He took Bread from the Baldock
Bakers frequently who, taking him at an advantage, put out his
Eyes and after hanged him upon a Knoll in Baldock Field. He made
them at his Exit but one single Request, which they granted: that
he might have his Bow put into his Hand, and wherever his Arrow
fell he should be buried, which happened to be in Weston churchyard'. The curious will find other versions, some of them improbably
embellished, in Gerish's *Hertfordshire Folk Lore*. If there is a temptation to dismiss Jack o' Legs as no more than the product of wish-
ful thinking among the medieval poor, it should perhaps be added
that Gerish found 'Jack's cave' marked on a map of 1620 and reports
that it was said to have been similar to Royston cave, though un-
decorated, by those who had seen it before it was filled in about 1850.
Perhaps Jack o' Legs had some origin in fact.

South-eastwards from Weston the lane leads to Walkern, passing
on the way Hall's Green with its very rural Rising Sun. Walkern
stands along the shallow valley of the little River Beane which once
drove the mill at the lower end of the street. The street itself is
pleasantly varied, timber-and-plaster mingling with later brick. At
the north end a good Georgian house is made more distinctive by
its octagonal and somewhat older dovecote. Halfway along the street
is the White Lion, two hundred years old externally, probably four
hundred years old inside. The church stands across the ford from
the village, half hidden behind a screen of limes. Externally it looks
mainly fourteenth century, but its interior shows a much earlier
origin. The crude south arcade is early Norman or, perhaps, late
Saxon. The monuments include a fine thirteenth-century knight in
marble (in remarkably good condition for so early a date), and two
brasses, one a palimpsest. A mile across the fields are traces of a
motte-and-bailey, but little is known of the Lanvalei family who
in about 1200 lived there.

Perhaps the most remarkable thing about Walkern is its name.
The 'aern' as in Totternhoe is Anglo-Saxon for a building, not a
'haws', which meant a dwelling but rather a structure used for a

particular purpose. The 'walk' refers to a process in wool-cloth making, the treading or fulling of the cloth so that absorbent 'fuller's earth' would remove the natural grease. An 'aern' built specially for such a purpose and noteworthy enough to name the settlement suggests that Saxon village life was less self-sufficient than has been assumed. Clearly the 'walk-aern' supplied the needs of more than the local villagers who, anyway, would have made their own cloth. Could it have been the centre for a large estate? Benington, a royal residence in Saxon times, is only two miles away. Or could there have been here an early industrial centre supplying the needs of Londoners?

Much later in its history Walkern came into the national eye with one of the last trials for witchcraft. On 4 March 1712, at the prompting of an hysterical and spiteful girl and more than a dozen credulous locals, seventy-year-old Jane Wenham was tried at Hertford Assizes and found guilty of the 'felony of witchcraft', and sentenced to death. A secondary assumption that she had by occult means contributed to the demise of her late husband was not pressed. The story, which Gerish tells in detail, was made distinctive by the persistence of superstition—shared apparently by Sir Henry Chauncy, the historian and Recorder of Hertford, who committed the old woman to gaol—and by the determined efforts of those who had come to discredit such odd and often locally convenient manifestations. The battle was fought on a national scale in a multitude of pamphlets and it did not end at the trial at which the judge, Mr Justice Powell, all but ordered the jury to acquit the woman only to find that 'the same Ignorance and Superstition which had instigated her accusers to apprehend her, operated in the minds of twelve men, sworn to do justice; and they, to their eternal shame, found her guilty'. Mr Justice Powell was not, however, the man to be overruled; he persuaded Queen Anne to grant a free pardon, and a sympathetic local landowner, realising that old Jane Wenham could not safely return to 'such a barbarous parish as she lived in', provided her with a cottage in which she lived 'soberly and inoffensively' for her remaining twenty years. The publicity the event aroused contributed to the repeal of the laws against witchcraft in 1736.

A left-hand turn a mile south of Walkern leads to much-photographed Benington. Certainly the black and white cottages and the Bell, an alehouse since before 1693, grouped about the pond at the upper end of the long, tilting green merit Pevsner's 'almost perfect'. The church, half-way down the green, possesses two good medieval

tombs and a brass, but its originally thirteenth-century work is rather too restored. Behind it, in the grounds of the great house, known as in several villages hereabouts as the Lordship, is the mound of a Norman castle with traces of walls; but they, and the nearby once-Georgian house, have been embellished with a spurious Normanness. The motte is believed to mark the site of the earlier residence of Berthulf, King of Mercia, who in 851 lost London to the Danes. The Domesday figures suggest that Benington saw too much of the Norman army. All that seems far away from the Benington of today.

Three gently undulating miles south is Watton-at-Stone, deriving its name of 'woad town' from the continued use of the ancient plant-dye into Saxon times, and its suffix from a Roman road that once linked Verulamium and Braughing. Watton's slightly winding street is, like Walkern's, mixed: Victorian cottage rows intermingled with earlier plaster and timber, and among them gabled Watton Hall, built about 1520, and the Bull and the George and Dragon, both probably seventeenth century. Watton church stands rather out of the village; it is very thoroughly embattled and somewhat thoroughly restored, possessing six brasses, a rather odd monument with kneeling figures that, by facing into the church, have their legs cut off by the wall, and several of the marble floor slabs that are often overlooked but sometimes appear more dignified than more elaborate memorials.

Watton's show-piece stands half-way along its street: an early nineteenth-century pump, now handle-less but so generously shaped that one suspects that it must in its day have drawn up some more convivial liquid than mere water. The later shelter to it, no doubt welcomed by the villagers in bad weather, commemorates a local celebrity who served in Egypt in 1882 and was at the battle of El Kebir—episodes that seem almost as remote from present-day Watton as the Conquest.

Another way through this region south of the Baldock–Royston section of Icknield is to take the lane that climbs across Therfield Heath and then follow the meandering crest-top way through Therfield, Kelshall, Sandon and Wallington. All four are spread about hill-tops on which, in contrast to the open fieldscape tilting away below them, many trees are gathered. The villages look at first glance somewhat random places, their mixtures of cottages—several of them of thatch-and-plaster for eastward flint is less used—are not

grouped tidily in lane-side rows but appear to have been sited more to fit the sudden twists of the lane or to avoid an abrupt drop of a hillside. Even so, the sites of all four were known to the Romans, their cemetery near Kelshall being still called Deadman's Hill. The house-name of Tuthill in Therfield recalls a Saxon look-out point, while Metley Hill north of Wallington was once 'Mete-hlaw', the meeting hill for the hundred. Both Sandon and Therfield have medieval mottes, that at Sandon having later ignominiously served as a windmill tump.

Therfield's Rectory is perhaps the most interesting building. Half of it is as early as about 1450 and was the manor-house in which was born Lord Berners, sometime minister to Henry VIII and translator of Froissart's *Chronicles*. Indirectly he is the source of those stirring fragments we remember from fourteenth-century history, notably young Richard II's: 'Sirs, I will be your chief and captain', to Wat Tyler's 'leaderless rabble'—which, oddly, none of the eye-witness accounts mentions. Indeed, reading Berners' Froissart now makes one wonder whether, at the dramatic moments both enjoyed recounting, the participants would have had the timing or the opportunity to express themselves in such quotable phrases. But, then, Froissart was concerned to win the favour of a royal patron—his chronicle was dedicated to Richard II—and the idea of translating him was suggested to Berners by Henry VIII, so perhaps we should not expect rigid accuracy.

Both Sandon's and Wallington's hill-top churches are notable. Sandon's is slightly the older, having been built late in the fourteenth century while the Perpendicular style was still softened by lingering traces of the Decorated. Wallington church, entered by a good porch, is mainly fifteenth century but most of its windows are not of the usual, rather rigidly traceried 'Perp' style; instead they hint of lancet-shaped lights set in neat, four-centre arches and so give a lighter, less formal appearance. Both churches have retained their old benches and screens, and Wallington has something of an oddity in a family pew—though the local 'family' cannot have been very impressive people for it is a rather humble example.

The quiet, expansive fields reaching away below Wallington give the cluster of houses about the church a feeling of apartness ... which is perhaps why 'George Orwell' made his home there. As a writer Orwell was, and has remained, a little apart for all his attempts to experience and understand the way of life of those of a very different background from his own. Son of a government

official in Bengal, educated at Eton via a scholarship, for a while in the Indian Police, a strong sense of social responsibility caused him during the 1930s to live among and write about tramps and drop-outs (*Down and Out in London and Paris*) and unemployed Lancashire workers (*The Road to Wigan Pier*). His sympathies urged him into the Spanish Civil War in an amateur, ill-equipped, anti-Franco force; the experience led to *Homage to Catalonia* with its cynical view of Russian participation. After such experiences and in declining health he withdrew to quiet Wallington where he kept the village store while writing his gentle satire *Animal Farm* and his disturbing vision of the political future, *1984*. Perhaps in Wallington it is better to remember the man behind the books with his concern for the less fortunate and for the 'little man' endangered by the all-powerful state. And the man and his ideas are ever and again recalled by many who have read little of his work: the date *1984* has become mental shorthand of threatening significance while the final dictum of *Animal Farm*'s politically triumphant pigs —'All animals are equal, but some animals are more equal than others'—has become a twentieth-century proverb. One day perhaps another of his books will be reread: *Coming up for Air*. A sociologically inclined historian writing a study of the thirties in a few decades' time may discover in it that society then comprised not only the workers and the middle-class but also the in-betweens. *Coming up for Air* is not a masterpiece, but few writers have written of the often overlooked in-betweens as shrewdly and as sympathetically.

From Wallington a lane leads southwards to the Cottered road. It passes through part of Rushden, a few cottages among which is the Moon and Stars, long, low and probably three hundred years old. For most of Rushden, a surprising, out-of-the-way place, one has to take a winding by-lane. After the rather scattered villages of the hill-tops, Rushden is so compact that its cottages, most of them thatched, seem almost jostling one another to keep their places along the twisting lane. Between them can be seen a larger, brick-and-timber house apparently of Tudor origin, and at the end of a dipping lane of more thatched cottages the church stands a little apart on an abrupt rise among the fields. The nave and tower are small-village fifteenth century; the white brick chancel is a Victorian remodelling. Beyond it, in its park, is the local great house built about 1700 but brought up to date in the 1930s.

Southwards, with a distant glimpse of the fine restored post mill above Cromer on the way, lies Cottered in a more level fieldscape.

First the thatched and weather-boarded Bell, an inn since before 1700, then the larger of the two greens with the houses set around it and half-hidden by great trees, and Cottered Lordship, built in about the 1480s and added to two hundred years later, behind its moat, and along the lane to Cromer the church. This is large-village Perpendicular in impression though much of the tower is a century older. It is light, spacious, dignified but, even with St Christopher to welcome the visitor, a little chill. In these fifteenth-century churches one is less aware of an impression of locality and individuality than in many of the earlier village churches. In the churchyard lies Sir James Cantlie, founder of the Royal Society of Tropical Medicine, for whose services to the China of Sun-Yat-Sen the Chinese government of 1926 set up the memorial in the church.

From Cottered the A 507 leads to Buntingford, which has one of the most interesting of main streets, not perhaps as obviously attractive as West Wycombe's but showing about every variation of small-scale architecture from the sixteenth century onwards. There are many timber-and-plaster houses with their 'overhangs'; among them eighteenth-century neat brick fronts, some enlivened with pilasters and decorative door-frames, tell of the prosperity of a couple of centuries ago. The street, which is a half-mile stretch of Ermine Street, ends with as fine a quadrangle of almshouses as is to be found. Built in 1684, it may have been designed under the eye of Sir Christopher Wren, for its founder, Seth Ward, was a personal friend of Sir Christopher, and was successively Bishop of Exeter and Salisbury as well as a noted mathematician and an astronomer. Ward was born at nearby Aspenden and, as the inscription on his 'hospital' says, began his education 'in ye free-school of Buntingford', a good daily walk from his home.

Near the almshouses is Buntingford's church, built in the 1620s on the Greek cross plan but apparently seeking to retain hints of the more traditional English styles; the apse and porch were added later. Inside is a brass showing the place as it was originally, complete with its first vicar in the pulpit. It was built as a chapel-of-ease to Buntingford's original church a mile away at Layston, for Buntingford is one of those villages that migrated from their earlier, agricultural site to gain part of their livelihood from the main-road traffic. Layston church still stands half-hidden by trees on its hill-top, roofless, forlorn and yet still retaining its ancient dignity.

Buntingford's street, the A 10, offers a convenient end to this

route; but if time allows there are Aspenden and Westmill along a loop road.

At first glance Aspenden looks a little suburban; it is more interesting along the lane which ends at its church, notable for two monuments: that to the brothers Freman, c. 1635, one of whom was Lord Mayor of London, and both of whom hold skulls; and that of Sir Robert Clifford who won Henry VII's uneasy favour only to try, a few years later, to get Perkin Warbeck into his place.

To a school that was held in Aspenden Hall came in 1818 young Thomas Babington Macaulay with his phenomenal verbal memory already well developed. (He had written a 'Universal History from the Creation' before he was eight and later claimed that he could memorise the whole of *Pilgrim's Progress* if he wished.) With such a gift, learning of the early nineteenth-century pattern came easily to him and he made rapid progress. That gift, too, helped him when in 1830 he entered Parliament for, though not such an impressive speaker as his writings might suggest, he could often floor his opponents by quoting from memory a wide range of authoritative statements. Whether his gift helped him as an historian is more open to question; he used it not so much as a basis for investigating historical causes and effects but rather as a prop to pre-conceived ideas and these essentially the conventional 'whig' ones of his day. He was, as a modern commentator puts it, 'brutally clear in his convictions'; in his *History*, says another, he 'explains all opposition to whig principles by the folly and knavery of their opponents'. Hardly the historian to appeal to today's more cautious practitioners; modern historians ride their hobby horses at a discreet trot, never at Macaulay's vigorous gallop. Yet, though his judgments may be questioned and the sweeping vigour of his writing has lost much of its appeal—but how well it fitted the mood of Victorian Britain! —he, more than any earlier historian, saw British history as a whole, and conveyed his vision in language that made history a popular subject if not to the masses at least to the middle classes of his day. Though nowadays more often quoted to have his assumptions questioned or condemned, his influence still underlies much of what our history books taught us at school.

Westmill, a little south of Aspenden and also just off the A 10, composes itself photogenically around a square green complete with well-house, and along a street leading to its once-Saxon church among chestnut trees. It must be confessed, however, that its primness is a little self-conscious, hinting that it is more a place of retired

country-lovers and those who are willing to commute from their carefully restored (and internally modernised) cottage homes. There is scarcely a house in the village which is not appropriately neat and well cared for, and many are delightful. (It is not every village which has its post office in a dignified Georgian house while a thatched cottage serves as the museum of local bygones.) To listen and observe from a corner seat in the homely public bar of the Sword in Hand will, however, reassure that there are still locally born Westmillers about.

The village has certainly spruced itself up since Charles Lamb came there to visit the cottage, Button Snap (probably Lamb's own name for it), at nearby Cherry Green, which he had inherited: 'When I journeyed down to take possession, and planted my feet on my own ground, the stately habits of the donor descended upon me, and I strode (shall I confess the vanity?) with larger paces over my allotment of three-quarters of an acre with its commodious mansion in the midst, with the feeling of an English freeholder that all betwixt sky and centre was my own.' The neat, thatched cottage is now cared for by the Royal Society of Arts in memory of him though ironically Lamb, unlike many of today's locals, had not the means to commute from London and so never lived in his 'hearty, homely, loving Hertfordshire'.

TEN

Beyond Royston

If geographers did not assert that the Chilterns reached their north-eastern limit at Hitchin or at Baldock, they would certainly insist that beyond Royston they should be renamed the East Anglian Heights. That name has a modern, school-text-book sound to it and unquestionably the Icknield Way, singular as it began, goes on another half-dozen miles, all but the first mile and a half from Royston a gentle grassy track as remote as any in southern England. And to its south the chalk hills persist though their contours are subdued and they reach to a skyline broken more often by hedges than by woods. Thanks to the ravages of the third Ice Age, man has long been able to tame these hills. Southwards from the last few miles of Icknield stretches a land of wide corn fields swelling out of shallow valleys, gentle, quiet and productive. It is more the ending of the Chilterns than the beginning of the haphazard landscapes of East Anglia.

For our last journey it would not be inappropriate to take one of the main roads to London, for though—perhaps guided by uncon-scious escapism—we have tended to ignore the fact, the proximity of London has played a large part in man's activities in the Chilterns from Roman times. Saxon Londoners, as we have noticed in passing, looked to this eastern region for much of their food and drink; through the medieval centuries and on into at least Stuart times the western woods provided fuel as well and, still later, furniture; and for the past five hundred years Londoners have sought and found sites for homes in all the more accessible parts of the Chilterns, in-creasingly during the last century. Lying across the routes from the capital to the North and the Midlands, the Chiltern area has seen and often benefited from the increasing traffic. So it is appropriate that our last journey should take a Londonward road.

A main road is, however, for people in a hurry. For those who wish to see, the more leisurely B 1368 is much more suitable. We

shall be following a route long known to the stage-coaches which still retains for much of its length the milestones their drivers reckoned by, the first milestones set up in England. They are suitably impressive, being embellished with the crescent badge of Trinity Hall, Cambridge, for they were erected in 1725 in belated accordance with the wishes of two Fellows who, a full century earlier, had often travelled this way to London. If the motorist starts along the road where it leads southwards from the hamlet of Bridgefoot three miles east of Royston, he will pass one of these milestones appropriately at the crossing of the Icknield Way, once more a gentle green lane. The next is in the dip before the road climbs to Barley, the only considerable hill that the stage-coaches had to tackle.

Though Ermine Street through Buntingford and Royston claimed much of the coach traffic for Cambridge, the B 1368 persisted as a recognised and slightly shorter route. Well into the 1800s coaches graced with such names as The Greyhound and The Lord Nelson coped with its gentle gradients while their passengers, like today's, could look over the sweeping fields or note the plaster-and-timber cottages they passed. The fare from London to Puckeridge was five shillings, to Cambridge ten shillings which, even allowing for the very different value of money, seems not excessive for conveying only half a dozen people at a time. Possibly the coach proprietors expected to make more profit from carrying mail. In 1814 postage on letters cost 4 pence up to 15 miles, 6 pence for 30 miles, 11 pence for 250 miles, 15 pence for 600 miles and 1 penny for every 100 miles thereafter, 'letters to and from Scotland $\frac{1}{2}$ penny more'. Mail-carrying looks a profitable business though, since the Napoleonic War was in progress, the operators relaxed their charges for some correspondents: 'Letters to Soldiers and Sailors, if single, charged 1 penny only'. No doubt the people of the time could interpret that ambiguous statement and knew whether the letters or the Soldiers and/or Sailors were to be single.

Barley is often said—sometimes by people who should know better —to owe its name to the grain. It would not be inappropriate if it did, as the fields about the village testify; but the name comes from the Anglo-Saxon 'burgen-leah', the 'burial clearing', and in confirmation the remains of a Roman cemetery have been found nearby. Barley's main street has several overhanging cottages and a Tudor town house built about 1530 probably by Henry VIII's Archbishop of Canterbury, William Warham, who had been a local boy. The house—it retains its original external staircase—'hath been tyme

out of mynde used and ymploied for the keeping of maides mar-
riages therein, and for the hangeing up of the Town Arms therein,
and for the chief inhabitants there to mete and consult'; it was also
used at one time as a school and, in the days when each village was
expected to provide for its own poor, as the workhouse.

The best-remembered house in Barley is the Fox and Hounds and
that because of its signboard. The figures of huntsmen, hounds and
fox make their way across the street by a gallows sign, one of the
few remaining from what were common sights in most towns until
banned in Charles II's time as liable to be a danger. The inn is suitably old—though it started life as a farmhouse, being converted to
the Waggon and Horses in 1797 when, befitting an inn on a coaching
road, it had stabling for thirty-two horses. The original Fox and
Hounds stood farther along the street but was burnt down in 1950
and the licence, sign and name were subsequently transferred to
their present site—and if a purist would think to disapprove of
such a means of preserving them in a suitable context he will feel
less inclined to after experiencing the house's welcome.

Near the inn stands the old village lock-up, reputed to date from
Stuart times. It looks well cared for and, if it is on its original site,
its position on the T-junction suggests that it might also have served
as a shelter for the village constable, that under-paid, untrained and
part-time officer who was supposed to maintain order in the village
before regular police forces began to be set up in the 1840s. In a
village like Barley on a then-busy main road the village constable's
job must at times have been testing ... which perhaps explains why
some early references accuse village constables of snoozing away
their watch in their 'watching hut' or hiding there when trouble
threatened.

From Barley the road curves through a park to Barkway with its
street twisting gently down-hill. The Saxons named it 'way over
the hill' suggesting that they approached from the south, which is
the better way. Viewed from its lower end Barkway's street is a
mixture of seventeenth-, eighteenth- and early nineteenth-century
houses, some tiled, some thatched, some of brick, some of plaster,
and one with its overhang dated 1687. The imaginative visitor could
well visualise the stage-coaches rattling up it, while the more prac-
tical-minded might catch the significance of a small, one-storeyed
building with an unexpected chimney half hidden by a sycamore.
This is the village bath-house presented, as the worn lettering tells,
in 1867 by a local benefactor (who also built the almshouses oppo-

site): a reminder that not so long ago bathrooms were very much a luxury and villagers had either to use a tin tub in the scullery, make their way to the nearest town with a public baths or go without. No doubt other villages similarly benefited from a wealthy resident's determination to give practical effect to the maxim that 'cleanliness is next to Godliness', but their bath-houses have been destroyed as unnecessary. Barkway's should be preserved; one day it might become a minor show-piece.

Barkway church, along a side street, was rather over-restored in 1861; the oldest parts date from the thirteenth century and there are some fragments of a fifteenth-century Jesse window. Once the church possessed a set of rare acoustic jars—medieval attempts at amplifiers —embedded in its chancel walls; but these have now disappeared. Opposite is the manor-house, originally Stuart though with something of medieval haphazardness.

From Barkway's street two roads offer detours, each of interest. That to the west from opposite the eighteenth-century Chaise and Pair leads to Reed; it gives fine views northwards over the tilting, unhedged fields, to the wide plain reaching out to Cambridge and beyond. Reed village is an odd place that should one day attract the attention of archaeologists. It is within a mile of Ermine Street and Roman traces have been found; indeed, the curious plan of the place—it is a series of short, straight lanes forming rectangles— suggests a Roman town though none is known to have been on the ridge-top site. Perhaps Reed may be an example of those semi-military, semi-civilian settlements about which, as yet, little is known: areas set aside for retired Roman legionaries where each was allocated a plot of ground (which the Roman mind would have insisted on being rectangular) to farm and so make what 'pension' he could. As yet the possibility has not attracted expert investigation.

Dotted along Reed's brief streets is a mixture of houses, cottages, a farm or two, and the village inn, The Cabinet, weather-boarded and tiled. An inn is known to have existed in Reed in 1657 and The Cabinet could well be the same house. By 1806 it had acquired its unusual name the origin of which has been lost—though the landlord will, on occasion, offer his own suggestion.

Reed church, nearly outside the village to the south, has been almost too well cared for. Rather unexpectedly it has, through the changes of nearly a thousand years, retained the Saxon 'long-and-short' external corners to its nave.

For the oddest of Reed's sights the visitor has to hunt. There are

around the place two artificial mounds, one enjoying the name of Periwinkle Hill, and no less than six moats, all still to be investigated and dated. So many fortifications in one square mile need some explanation; dare one mention the 'adulterine castles' of King Stephen's time? Reed's situation close to Ermine Street and yet screened from it by a half-mile of wood and brush would have been an ideal spot for those who 'plundered and burned' in those lawless days when 'Christ slept and all His Saints'.

It is time to return to Barkway.

From the south end of Barkway's street, near what was once a toll-house, a lane to the east leads through Anstey. This is another odd place, rather scattered. At the north is a small green with the well still furnished with winch, chain and bucket. (Nearby is a street named 'Cheapside'; it would be interesting to know if the name first recorded in 1676 was the former market-place.) Below, where the road twists into a shallow valley, stands the church and the manor-house (rebuilt recently); and on across a languid stream is the rest of the place. The whole gives the impression that Anstey was once more populous. In Norman times it possessed a castle; the massive motte on which it stood, one of the largest in the country, is in the wood behind the church.

The church is very impressive and very puzzling. It is said to have been founded by Richard de Anestie in the fourteenth century, but much of the fabric is clearly a full century earlier than that. Even Pevsner, who finds the building 'architecturally interesting', is unsure about it; the central tower, he says, 'seems' to be Norman but is of so late a date that he has to suggest that, medieval builders being ignorant of the architectural periods of later historians, Norman work was still being built in 1200, fifty years after the last Norman king had given way to the first Plantagenet. There seems little doubt that the chancel and the transepts were built about 1270 and that the tower joining them is work of a century earlier, and yet all appears to have been built at the same time.

Perhaps the answer to Pevsner's uncertainty and to many others' puzzlement is to be found in Mrs V. Pritchard's *English Medieval Graffiti*, a book that will open the eyes of many who think they know about old churches. Mrs Pritchard, in search of those interesting and ancient scratchings that are to be found in many old churches, studied Anstey's collection. It is mainly on the tower piers, and it depicts arms, crests, the kind of cart used to transport armour and weapons, and other military subjects more suited to a castle than a

church. From this Mrs Pritchard suggests that the stones (and presumably the whole arches of which they are part) may have come from Anstey castle; and in support of the suggestion she mentions a local legend that the castle was destroyed to build the church. Mrs Pritchard has also collected what little history can tell of the place: that in King John's time its owner, Nicolas de Anstie, sided with the barons against the King, that he was in 1218 ordered by Henry III to destroy the outer defences of his castle, that on Anstie's death in 1225 Henry seized the place and handed it to the Archbishop of Canterbury for safe-keeping. Thereafter history tells little, though Henry VIII granted the place—the actual castle or the manor and its revenues?—to each of his first three wives in turn.

If it is not presumptuous for a non-expert to judge such technical matters, Mrs Pritchard's theory has plausibility. The castle is known to have been of great strength which suggests a stone structure and, indeed, Mrs Pritchard found a piece of clunch on the motte similar to that used in the church. Assuming that Henry III's order of 1218 was carried out, what happened to the rest of the stone? If—which is most unlikely at so early a date—the castle had been used by the locals as a convenient quarry, surely some fragments would have survived. But if a descendant of the Ansteys had in about 1270 obtained permission to found a monastery at his ancestral home and nearby were the remains of the castle's 'slighted' outer defences with much of the Norman stonework capable of re-use, including some more or less complete round-headed arches ... To be sure, the result would to thirteenth-century eyes have looked a little old-fashioned, but not more so than hundreds of other churches which then retained far more of their Norman builders' work than they do now. It may be that at Anstey legend was based on fact.

Much more could be said about Anstey church, but the visitor should see for himself—and not overlook the misereres in the chancel, as always very medieval in idea, and the ancient chests in the vestry, and the two tally-sticks surviving from the days before accountancy meant book-keeping. And as he leaves he should note the lychgate, five hundred years old and with a part walled up to make the village lock-up. At least it was used as a lock-up (or 'cage' as such temporary prisons were often called) in the 1820s for in December 1831 it had to be repaired after Thomas Edwards, locked in for disorderly conduct, had escaped by pushing down a wall. It seems that Edwards was not the only disturber of the local peace. A few years later Thomas Barker requested in his will that 'you will

bury me outside the Cage; many a time have I been shut inside and now I want to be outside'. His wish was granted and he lies near the lock-up door.

The position of this door, looking not upon the village but into the churchyard, suggests that the lock-up may have served another purpose. It may have been used at times as a 'watching hut' from which, through the nights following a burial, a watchman kept a look-out for 'resurrection men'. The increasing interest in anatomy during the eighteenth century created a demand for newly-dead corpses to study and dissect, and some village churches found it necessary to forestall the activities of body-snatchers gruesomely intent on satisfying the demand. The position of the door to Anstey's lock-up suggests that when it was fashioned some time in the eighteenth century the possibility of its use as a 'watching hut' may have been in local minds.

From Anstey a lane leads to Great and Little Hormead or, better still, there is a shorter, mile-long footpath across the fields. Great Hormead's main street has several houses between two and three hundred years old, some thatched, some timbered, some plastered, and many set in gardens with fine trees—it is one of the greenest of village streets. Little Hormead consists only of a few houses about a small, mostly Norman church, narrow and plain. It has a rarity in a wooden door decorated with an elaborate pattern of ironwork as old as the church itself. Guide-books comment, sometimes at length, on fifteenth-century woodwork; Little Hormead's door dates from soon after 1100. The ironwork holding together the ancient wood is very strange. There are in the twisting, interlocking lines hints of those 'strap patterns' enjoyed by the Saxons—but it cannot be as old as that. A note in the church suggests that Saxon (i.e. English) workers might have been employed in the building and draws attention to some of the simply carved stonework as hinting of Saxon motifs; and, in doing so, reminds us that when Little Hormead's church was being built the Conquest was only a generation away. And only the chancel of a village church—in Little Hormead of slightly later date than the nave—was provided at the Church's expense; the nave was the responsibility of the parishioners. In this church it is possible that the locals of about 1100 took their responsibility literally. There is a home-made look about the place; and local effort must have survived into the fifteenth century to judge by the crudely fashioned roof timbers of that date when the church had to be re-roofed.

While on the subject of odd survivals, those interested might like to visit Wyddial, two miles to the northwest of Hormead. The rarity there, again in the church, is more recent than Little Hormead's but in its way as unusual. It was the outcome of a wish on the part of the lord of the manor to be very modern—but in 1532, a time when the traditional stone for larger buildings was giving way to the new-fangled brick ... so when the north aisle of Wyddial church was to be remodelled to serve as the family chapel the result was an oddly red and indisputably Tudor contrast to the older stone arcade to the south. In itself the work is attractive, and clearly the brickwork has been shaped to match the stone; yet there lingers a feeling of asser-tion, the Tudor new intruding into the old. The screens which en-close the chapel are of a century later still but seem less out of place; and there are in this church two brasses, both of Tudor date, the one in the chancel being a remarkably detailed piece of work.

On by lanes or footpaths to Braughing. The country hereabouts is gentle and undramatic; and the path from Hormead leads past an odd mound—Bummers Hill—perhaps Roman, and two of the moats which are so plentiful in eastern Hertfordshire and about which, as they have not yet been subjected to expert examination, the walker can let his imagination play.

As has been mentioned, the name Braughing comes from an early Saxon tribal name. It is, by the way, pronounced 'Braffing', and if a visitor feels inclined to complain that that is not obvious, he should try his tongue around some of the earlier spellings: Brea-hingas (pre-Conquest), Brachinges (1070), Brakinghe (1100), Brawgh-ing (1550), Brauhing (1770). But however spelt or pronounced Braughing is for most motorists the street along the B 1368, a pleasant street with a collection of varied houses and some good trees. True Braughing, however, lies on the slope rising up from the fords across the little River Quin. There is the ancient, finely-towered church and on three sides of the churchyard the older houses mainly of timber and plaster, some with pargetting, and the brick-and-timber (and restored) Old House in which, by the will of a former owner, the local poor couples held their wedding reception —and one room in it formerly held the 'bride bed' thoughtfully pro-vided. Nearby more houses, some old, some new, form the Square— for King Stephen, no doubt in one of his less harassed moments, granted the town a market.

The architecture of the church was once all Early English but now only the chancel and perhaps the nave arcades are of so early

8. Fifteenth-century school, Ewelme

FOR YOUNG AND OLD

9. Seventeenth-century almshouses, Mapledurham

VILLAGE INNS

31. *The Three Horse-shoes, Radnage*

a date; the present nave dates from the fifteenth century and the north aisle was enlarged in 1638 (at which time it served as a school for the local poor children). The roofs are contemporary. The south porch, also fifteenth-century work, is large and impressive; it was intended for gatherings to discuss local matters (which earlier would have met in the church itself) and for special village occasions, such as when at a wedding the groom announced what he intended to bequeath to his bride should he pre-decease her (and were in the Wife of Bath's mind, no doubt, when she mentioned her matrimonial adventures: 'Housbondes at chirche-dore I have had fyve').

Braughing is one of those places where an old custom might be expected to linger—and one does. On 2 October the church bells are rung, first a single bell as though tolling for a funeral, then the full eight bells pealing as if for a wedding. The custom has its origin in an event concerning Mathew Wal, one of Braughing's former benefactors. The story tells that in 1561 when a young man and engaged to be married, he was taken ill and shortly afterwards died. The funeral was arranged for 2 October. Wal's home being in that part of Braughing along the main road, the coffin had to be carried across the footbridge beside one of the fords—that in Fleece Lane is said to be the one—and on the way one of the bearers slipped and the coffin fell with a bump on to the bridge. As the bearers were about to lift it again, a knocking was heard coming from inside the coffin. The lid was lifted and 'to everyone's amazement the corpse sat, rubbed his eyes and spoke'. Mathew Wal was hurried home, nursed back to full health, and the following spring walked again along Fleece Lane with his bride on his arm while the church bells pealed. He lived another thirty-four years and in his will left several bequests to the local poor. The double bell-ringing, first the tolling, then the pealing, is said to have been kept up ever since in memory of his 'miraculous recovery'.

There is no monument to Wal in the church—he was buried in the churchyard apparently without a stone to mark his grave—but there are other things to see, including some fifteenth-century benches decorated with carved animals and a monument to the brothers Brogrove (circa 1625) on which besides the reclining figures, an angelic Vanity blows soap bubbles at Father Time, and a memorial to John Mellish, M.P., who in 1798 died from wounds inflicted by footpads (at Hounslow, not locally).

From Braughing it is little more than a mile to the A 10; but before taking the homeward way there is Puckeridge (the 'Goblin's

Ridge' of the Saxons who were great believers in sprites, demons and other unearthly but sometimes rather earthy beings).

It is difficult not to feel sorry for Puckeridge. Its narrow, winding street has several timber and plaster 'overhanging' houses, but for too long the passing traffic has splashed their fronts with mud; at last a bypass, now under construction, is to give the place a chance. It deserves it, for Pepys liked it, staying sometimes at the Falcon—now the Crown and Falcon—at the corner of the road to Standon. Though externally the inn is much as Pepys knew it, he would probably recognise little of the inside with its twentieth-century attempts to provide an 'olde worlde' impression. Incidentally, in October 1662, he learnt there a piece of news which might make a modern historian speculate. 'Mr Brian with whom I supped, and was very good company and a scholar. He tells me that the Queen is with child, for that the coaches are ordered to ride very easily through the streets.' We must assume that Catherine of Braganza suffered a miscarriage for had she produced an heir to the throne, the Glorious and/or Bloodless Revolution of 1688 that put William and Mary on the English throne with all its consequences embellished by Whig historians would never have happened.

Puckeridge is another of those places on the main road which grew on the increasing travel during the seventeenth and eighteenth centuries. The original settlement was Standon, a mile to the southeast. Its parish was large, for Standon Lodge is a mile and a half away to the southeast while Standon Green End is more than two miles to the southwest. The parish church at the end of a wide street with some good Georgian houses is appropriately large. It is a striking building with its fine fifteenth-century tower (originally detached from the church), its impressive west porch, and its thirteenth-century chancel raised up a flight of steps from the nave. The nave is a Victorian reconstruction but it blends well with the older work.

Standon is a fitting place at which to end our wanderings along the Chiltern Ways. Like so many little places it has links with events that have gone into the making of England. Not far away a Roman villa stood, the Conqueror passed through it en route for London and the Crown, and there are traces of the earthworks of a medieval castle. Bright and hygienic as Standon now appears, chance has made it one of those places for which records are available for 1349, the year the Black Death struck. Standon's suffering can be summed up in one sentence. In the summer of 1348 thirty-two tenants mowed

their lord's hay, in 1349 the lord's hay was left to rot, twenty years later many of the village tenements were still unoccupied.

Standon's past is more visible in the church. There is the fine tomb to one of those wool-merchants who enriched themselves and incidentally helped their country during the great days of the late medieval wool trade: John Field of the 'Stapull of Caleys' who lent Henry VI the then-large sum of £2,000 for the defence of Calais. His brass shows him in merchants' dress and in place of a coat-of-arms he has a 'wool mark'. His son, who lies beside him, is shown wearing armour and he has a real coat-of-arms; he had, thanks to his father's wealth and business acumen, achieved the gentry. In the chancel is a later monument to Sir Ralph Sadleir who in 1547 had the thankless task of trying to arrange, against Scottish hostility, a marriage between nine-year-old Edward VI and five-year-old Mary, Queen of Scots. The negotiations ended in war, and above Sir Ralph's monument hangs the banner which the English forces won at Pinkie, almost the last armed contest before the English and Scottish crowns were united. That event is recalled by the nearby monument to Sir Ralph's son, Sir Thomas, who 'royally entertained' James I at Standon, the stop after Royston on his Scottish Majesty's route to London and the English throne. The Sadleirs' home, Standon Lordship, stands half a mile to the southwest and still retains some of the original Tudor work.

Nearly two hundred years later Standon briefly reappeared in history. On 15 September 1784 a young Italian, Vincenzo Lunardi, and his dog visited the place—or, more accurately, Standon Green End two miles to the southwest but still officially part of Standon. Lunardi and his dog arrived not on foot or by horse or coach; they arrived by balloon at the end of the first successful long-distance flight made in England by man (and presumably dog). They had travelled some thirty miles from London's Moorfields without mishap—though the story tells that over North Mimms the balloon came so near to grounding that Lunardi judged it necessary to lighten his load by dropping his pet cat into the arms of a passing countrywoman. It is a pity that history does not record their brief conversation.

Lunardi was, years later, buried in Standon church. Where his balloon had landed a stone was set up with a plaque recording that Lunardi 'after Traversing the Regions of the Air for Two Hours and Fifteen Minutes On this Spot Revisited the Earth' and so ended a 'Wondrous Enterprise Successfully Achieved by the Powers of

Chemistry and the Fortitude of Man ... which The Great Author of all Knowledge Patronising by His Providence the Invention of Mankind Hath Graciously Permitted to Their Benefit and His Own Eternal Glory'. That monument has now to be looked for—which is perhaps fitting. We of the Jet Age and the moon trip know that the ideas behind Lunardi's method of achieving flight were of much more limited application than he no doubt hoped, and we are less sure of God's part in such an enterprise. Sightseers' feet no longer tread a path across the field to where his stone stands half-hidden by weeds—which suggests that we consider Lunardi and his balloon-flight hardly worth remembering, even though he was one of those rare people who helped to make the impossible possible.

So, in the gently undulating fields about Standon, we come to the end of the journey, a journey which began at Icknield's start on the Thames at Goring all of 8,000 years ago and has ended with the first attempt in England at flying—to which we can add the modern road that has been constructed at Standon to help ease east–west motor traffic and the even newer bypass to nearby Puckeridge. We began at a time and place in which natural features shaped man's first steps towards today: the barrier of the Thames which had to be crossed, the thinly covered escarpment offering an easy route through a forested Britain, the easily cultivable Icknield strip encouraging the first efforts at husbandry; we have ended in a landscape that shows it has been tamed for two millennia and is being modified to suit present needs. And on the way we have enjoyed the subtly changing delights of the Chilterns ranging from the massive rise of the southern escarpment to the gently sweeping country beyond Royston, from the ever-haunting beechwoods to the open fields of the east, and interspersed with so many combes and bottoms and valleys that their variety seems endless. Ever and again we have glimpsed something of all that has happened within these hills to make them as they are; and, as in the Standon neighbourhood, often these glimpses have been the more telling because of the many juxtapositions reaching across centuries: Therfield's Neolithic barrow close to a very twentieth-century golf course, ancient Icknield passing a Stuart farmhouse, fields won from natural forest by Anglo-Saxon churls adjoining beechwoods planted for eighteenth-century landowners and nineteenth-century furniture-makers, a medieval church alongside an inn refronted to attract stage-coach passengers, a Roman road being bypassed by a motorway. Such

juxtapositions, and they are countless, give to the Chilterns a continuity perhaps clearer than anywhere else. That these chalk hills have witnessed and fostered man's activity for 8,000 years is to be seen by everyone with the ability to interpret what is before his eyes.

As we have seen many times, the Chiltern landscape, part natural, part man-made, is essentially one of partnership. Impressive though the hills are in their fine rise from the plain, they are on their dip slopes and in their valleys easy enough for man to have been able to use them, to create on them his varying patterns of field and wood and hedgerow. Neither man nor land dominates; there are no stretches of hillscape where man has had to destroy the original character to gain a livelihood, there are no areas so intractable as to have resisted cultivation. Over the whole region man and land have worked together to make the Chilterns as they are.

The results of man's working, and of his ways of thinking and believing, are to be seen in the villages and towns even more than in the landscape. There we have been able to see a little of the social patterns of different periods of the past, the varying notions of need and comfort, and sometimes expressions, not always to our taste, of individuality ... to which we should add the older houses that have been refurbished recently for, no doubt, some sociologist of the future will explain a people who built block towers reaching twenty storeys or more and at the same time delighted in homes fashioned out of a pair of 200-year-old labourers' cottages or the modest house of a village craftsman. More significant are the churches built for God by men who, like men of every age, had their strengths and weaknesses, their glimpses of beauty and their hunger for understanding. The Chiltern churches are for the most part architecturally modest, at times humble—but more than splendid cathedrals and impressive town-churches built by the wealthy they are essentially of and for the people who worshipped in them. Whatever our religious views, we must acknowledge a one-ness with those many generations for we, like them, know man's need for more than a material interpretation of life. The churches are much more than history in stone; they are expressions of the human striving for understanding, a striving which began before Icknield was trodden and will continue as long as man lives in the Chilterns.

And the Chilterns are of all time. The changes of the recent past have fortunately been accompanied by a growing awareness of the

dangers they can bring. The Chiltern character must be allowed to continue, but as a living entity, not as a museum piece or a playground. Those guardians of the 'Chiltern Area of Outstanding Natural Beauty', the Chilterns Standing Committee, are surely right when they say in their 'Plan for the Chilterns' that not only must the obvious attractions be preserved but also that 'the ecology of the area must be allowed to evolve in its own peculiar way. It must remain a living area where forestry and farming can be carried on in a robust and confident manner'. The age-old partnership between man and the hills must continue.

For Further Reading

Several of the books to which reference has been made have been mentioned in appropriate places in the text. For those readers who would wish to know more, it may be helpful to mention some fairly accessible books.

For the geology of the Chilterns a good concise introduction covering the southern half is J. T. Coppock's *The Chilterns* (Geographical Assocn, 1968), a study of the Ordnance Survey one-inch sheet No. 159. More detailed information is to be found in *Structure, Surface and Drainage in South-East England* by S. W. Wooldridge and D. L. Linton (George Philips, 1968), and R. L. Sherlock's *London and the Thames Valley* (H.M. Stationery Office, 1971).

For an outline of archaeology and early history G. J. Copley's *Archaeology of South Buckinghamshire* (Phoenix House, 1958) is a very readable and localised account, while the Chilterns are covered in Gordon J. Copley's *Archaeology of South-East England* (Phoenix House, 1958), which includes a gazetteer of the sites known up to the time of its writing and deals with early medieval topics that are sometimes overlooked. These books have to be supplemented by the more recent publications of the local Archaeological Societies; there are also the annual archaeological publications of H.M.S.O. which give useful summaries of the preceding year's work, especially of excavations undertaken in advance of road-building. For the specialised subject of Roman roads the 'Viatores' detailed *Roman Roads in the South-East Midlands* (Victor Gollancz, 1964), which deals very thoroughly with the Chiltern region, is essential.

For architecture Nikolaus Pevsner's books on the buildings of the counties are the most complete summaries of what is note-

worthy, particularly among the larger buildings. The earlier 'Little Guides' to the counties also give useful summaries mainly of church architecture, while the 'Companions into' Buckinghamshire, Hertfordshire, Oxfordshire often include supplementary matter and some accounts of the historically noteworthy residents of the places covered, as do also—if the reader is not troubled by the rather dated enthusiasm—Arthur Mee's books on the counties.

For local history the reader has two main sources: the many books on individual towns and villages that were for the most part written a half-century and more ago, and those of the last decade or so. The earlier ones, long out of print, have to be looked for in local libraries; though sometimes tending to concentrate on the local 'families' and their connections and on incidents linked with national history, they often include extracts from early documents and sometimes old residents' (i.e. mid-Victorian) recollections which would otherwise have been lost. The more recent local histories often delve more into the surviving records of the lives of the humbler people and so give the other, formerly overlooked side of the picture. Many of both kinds are very informative, but it would be invidious to single out some for special mention—and the reader will wish to find those covering places that interest him. To these should be added the booklets to be bought in several churches and the sheets sometimes on hand that tell visitors of the building's history. Slight though many of these are in appearance they are these days no longer merely concerned to claim the utmost antiquity for their subject or to recount improbable legends; they are often in their small compass authoritative works which also serve to draw attention to details which the visitor may otherwise miss. And such periodicals as *Chiltern Life* and *Hertfordshire Countryside* and *Thames Valley Countryside* should not be overlooked; though not pretending to be learned works, they often include local residents' recollections, items of family history and papers prompted by local concern which give interesting sidelights on particular places. Finally a remarkable book on an often overlooked county: Joyce Godber's *History of Bedfordshire* (1969). This is a detailed account built upon local happenings and local personalities and makes absorbing reading for those interested in social history. Published by the Bedfordshire County Council, it deserves to inspire other local authorities to produce comparable works.

Index

Figures in **bold type** indicate whole chapters or principal references.

'*p*' means *passim* (here and there), two or more mentions

© *Cassell & Co. Ltd.* 1973